CW00642803

A New Dawning

It All Starts with a Decision

Ann Guindi

A New Dawning

A self-published book by Ann Guindi with support from

Mirav Tarkka

www.amazon.com/author/mirav/tarkka
www.facebook.com/miravtarkka

First published in 2022

ISBN 9 798987 21 7245

Dedication

This book is dedicated to the readers and to all those who have ever had a false belief planted in your head that stopped you from reaching your full potential.

I want you to know that you can BE, DO or HAVE anything that you desire in your life. You just need to believe in yourself and make the decision to go after it.

Book Reviews

"I was so honoured to review a chapter of Anne's book. Her knowledge is so vast. She demonstrates how her personal experience has empowered her to help herself and others to grow into the best version of themselves."

Terry Levine | Business Consultant at Heartrepreneur®

"Reading this book and implementing the tools will help you gain confidence in your life and business. You will go from FEAR to FEARLSS."

Ferilicus Ong | Business Strategist | Founder of CRE8Value LLC

"This book is super insightful!... I love the clarity and breakdown of each term, how it relates, and real-life examples. Plus, such powerful graphics that really help me to visualise how NLP works in real life. So cool."

Brendan McCauley | Business Development Engineer at Growing Entrepreneur

"This book is awesome and will help so many people to make positive changes in their life."

Maria Elizabeth van Niekerk | CEO of Make Passive Money Now

"Ann's personal story is a powerful one, where fear controlled her, and kept her from living the life she was meant to live. You can literally feel Ann's pain as she relates a childhood where trauma and fear created her belief system and ruled her life for decades. Ann has the amazing ability to explain deep, complex issues with clarity and understanding. You can live vicariously through Ann's triumphant transformation, and even better still, Ann lays out an easy-to-follow system so you can make lasting change in YOUR life. This incredible work has my highest recommendation!"

Brent Webb | Acclaimed Mind Power Expert
www.SuccessSecrets.net

"This book really resonates with me as it will for others. Ann shows how you can rise above adversity and not be defined by others. This book will help many other people to rise up."

Parm Sran | Mindset Mentor | Author | Speaker

"It is clear that Ann has made significant breakthrough and her deepest desire is to reach back and help others do the same in their life and business! This book will change lives!

Noelle McGough | Co- Founder/CEO at
The Challenge Queens Event Agency

Ann's Story is so relatable and captivating, it pulled me right in…

Jola Crapanzano | Amazon Best Selling Author

Table of Contents

Part Two: Mission

Part Three: Moves

About the Author

Ann is a seasoned entrepreneur, having set up her first two London-based Montessori Day Nurseries in 2004 and 2007. She started her journey in personal development in 2009 having trained as a protégé student with the Coaching Academy and qualified as a Personal Performance and Business Coach. She is also a master Practitioner of Neuro Linguistic Programming (NLP), along with being a trained psychologist and counsellor.

Ann has a background in the National Health Service (NHS) as a children's nurse and health visitor. She wrote her first book back in 2014 whilst working as a parent coach, specialising in helping parents of under-fives to teach their child to sleep.

She currently works as a business confidence coach helping entrepreneurs to become more visible, find their voice to grow, and scale their business.

Contact Information:
Email: ann@believetoachievecoaching.com
Website: http://www.believetoachievecoaching.com
Connect with me on social media:
LinkedIn:
https://www.linkedin.com/in/ann-guindi-businesssuccesscoach/
Twitter: https://twitter.com/GuindiAnn
FB Business Page:
https://www.facebook.com/believetoachievecoaching/
Instagram: Ann Guindi - Business/Parent Coach

Introduction

I was 16 years old when I experienced a significant emotional event that changed the course of my life.

It happened during an Irish lesson. My Irish teacher used to always get people to stand up and read our book out loud to the class. I was barely able to read in English let alone Irish. I had dyslexia, but I did not know that at the time. I just thought I was a bit slow at learning. I would always try and sit at the back of the class in the hope that the teacher would run out of time and not get around to me. Most of the time that tactic did not work. I used to call this tradition the *creeping death* as I dreaded it so much. On this particular day, it was my turn to stand up and read. I could feel the FEAR building up inside me as my turn approached. My hands were sweating, my mouth was dry, my heart was beating out of my chest, and I was hoping that I would not faint. I had experienced this feeling many times as it was my constant unwelcome companion during my school years. I was very well-rehearsed at with performing in this state of fear and could run it very well in most situations of my life. It was my embedded enemy.

It came to my turn. I stood up and opened my month, but the words wouldn't come. I stuttered and stammered to try and get the words out. It was futile. In Irish, the teacher said, "*Suigh Sios, Aine, ta tu Amadan*", or "Sit down, Ann. You fool." The whole class laughed out loud. I felt *shame* and *hurt.*

What the teacher said to me that day had a profound impact on me as a vulnerable, shy and introverted teenager. At that moment I made a self-limiting decision about myself that I could not read in public and a formed a negative belief that I was stupid. That experience held me back for the next 25 years of my adult life.

In 1982 during a career guidance session, I was told that "I should become a nurse or a teacher as that is what is best for girls. I secretly always wanted to be a doctor and worked hard at school to achieve my goal of being a paediatrician, but my efforts didn't reflect my grades being a 'C' student. Again, I was told by teachers "I couldn't to study Physics or Chemistry as this was only for the 'A' students." Open to only those who met the standard, these students could go to the boy's school that did allow girls to access these subjects only if they were good enough and met the grade.

Those experiences led me to a lifelong feeling of not being 'good enough' or clever enough.

I lived most of my adult life in *fear* which stopped me from going after my hopes and dreams. I lived in the shadows, ducking, and diving trying to avoid any situation where I may be made to feel hurt again like that vulnerable teenager at school. I lacked confidence, had low self-esteem and was scared most of the time. I learned to stay in my comfort zone and would not attempt to put myself in any situation where I could be exposed. I let *fear* hold me back. This was a problem for me. A big problem as I felt stuck, I could not move forward and stayed in the same job for 15 years where it was safe.

You may be feeling the same way right now. You may believe that you can't change this is how you are. But it doesn't have to be that way. You have a choice. You can CHANGE. There is a solution, and this book will show you the way.

I wrote this book for those who feel stuck or trapped, in your job, your life, your relationships, whatever and wherever you feel you can't move on, because you lack the confidence and belief in yourself. You feel that you can't apply for a better job, or you can't study for that course you want as you might fail, but you would be wrong.

I was like you and then I found the solution. It came out of the blue. I was sitting beside someone at a table during a corporate dinner with my husband's job. I was making small talk as you do and I asked the man sitting next to me what his job was. He told me he was an NLP coach. I did not have a clue what that was, and I didn't want to appear stupid as I already felt that. Luckily, he was kind enough to elaborate and tell me that NLP stood for Neuro Linguistic Programming (NLP), and it is the study of how our thoughts affect our behaviour. Now that got my attention.

That night I went home and googled how to find an NLP training program. I signed up for an NLP Course in 2009 and the impact of that course set me on a new trajectory for my life. I was like a different woman after that experience. I learned so much about my thoughts, feelings, beliefs, values, behaviour and how I could change them. It was like an epiphany. I was so enlightened with this new knowledge that I went on to do the master practitioner training and that's when my life changed forever. As part of that training, I had my own breakthrough. I got rid of all my negative emotions, I smashed through all my limiting decisions and negative beliefs. I started my new life as an empowered woman.

This is my wish for every person that picks up this book that you can CHANGE your life. You just must decide you want it just like I did.

I want you to have a happier, healthier, and more prosperous life and to live life on your terms. You can Be, DO, HAVE your heart's desire if you BELIEVE you can ACHIEVE and change your life. You just must make the decision; a New Dawning is just around the corner.

Are you ready to decide to move forward?

PART ONE:

Mindset

CHAPTER 1

Values and Beliefs

"Beliefs become your thoughts,
Your thoughts become your words,
Your words become your actions,
Your actions become your habits,
Your values become your destiny."

Mahatama Gandhi

Introduction

I want to start this chapter by saying that I don't have any regrets in my life, and I never look back at the past as it does not serve us. I am a towards person and will always look towards the future and what I want to achieve in my life. All our experiences whether good or bad make us who we are today and give us our purpose in life to serve others if we so wish to. I really loved my life as a nurse and had the privilege of caring for many hundreds of children and families.

But I do believe that confidence and self-belief would have made my life much easier and less fearful. I have a positive outlook on life and my glass is always half full. I do not believe in talking about anything that is negative as it gives the negativity power. So, this book will focus on the positive and not the negative as this is what is important to me in life.

What is important to you in your life?

What is a Value?

Values are in essence what is important to us, they are high level generalisations that we adopt into our life. They can be described as a set of rules that we live by. In Neuro Linguistic Programming (NLP) we sometimes call them criteria.

A value can be a 'hot button' that drives your behaviour. Whatever you do in life is done in order to fulfil a value – even though you are unlikely to be consciously aware this 'hot button' is a value, as they sit deep in your unconscious mind.

Everything you do is a means to an end and this end is the fulfilment of a value. You do what you do to move towards pleasurable feelings or move away from something to avoid painful feelings.

I have always been a towards person as I have a positive mindset. My top value in life is and has always been my family. Every decision that I make in my life will be centred around the needs of my family. I wanted to be a good mother and spend time with my children when they were little. Even now as adults, I like being around my family. I am happiest when I am on holiday with my family making memories together. This value was formed from my own early childhood experiences, which were negative, but made me who I am today, a strong, driven, and successful woman. I don't entertain the past as I only look towards the future and never look back as it does not serve me.

Everything you do will move you a little towards fulfilling a pleasurable value and a little away from feeling a painful one. We feel good when we are successfully fulfilling our 'towards' values or avoiding our 'away from' values. For example, some may say, "I want to be happy." This is a 'towards' type of statement. While "I don't want to be unhappy," is an 'away' type of person statement.

The Value of Values

I always do a values elicitation exercise to find out what is important to you in your life and business. I am a business confidence coach and I help entrepreneurs to become more visible to grow their business.

Knowing your values enables you to:

- make better decisions, since you have greater awareness of what is truly important to you.
- be more in control of your actions and your emotions.
- recognise what you need to do to feel good.
- find lots of different ways of fulfilling them rather than the same old things as before.

We all have different values in given situations. What we value in our relationships may be different to our business.

The values exercise is integral to getting to know you and this is why I get you to complete this tool. I will always start with asking you this question:

Q. What's important to you about X, in your career, relationships, family, health and fitness, personal growth or business.

Changing Values

I am often struck by how many people that I work with do not put down money as a value. This may be the reason that many of you are not growing or scaling your business. It will often not be visible in the top three or can be missing completely. Many entrepreneurs have money blocks that need addressing. This is where I work with you to bring this awareness into your life and change your values to incorporate money.

Sometimes our values are misaligned or absent completely as mentioned above in the case of money. This often causes disagreements and incongruency. If you are a new start-up business, you may not yet have a value for money you simply value your product or idea. By changing their values, I help you look at your project as a business not just as a hobby. Some business owners, on the other hand, only have a value of money and will do anything to get it. These people can also change their values to include 'integrity' and 'compassion' to bring more balance into their business and attract more clients.

Setting the right foundations is important for your business.

Beliefs

Beliefs are generalisations we all make about the world and our opinions about it. They form the rules about what we can and cannot do.

We form our beliefs in our early childhood, they come from our parents, our religion, our culture, our peers, our education, and other influences like the media.

Values and beliefs are found deep down in our unconscious mind.

Beliefs that we adopt that limit the way we live our lives are called self-limiting beliefs. They fall into four categories.

1. Anything you can't feel – such as – I worry and doubt myself.
2. Negations – such as – I am too old/young.
3. Comparatives – such as – I'm not good enough, I can't attract enough clients.
4. Limiting decisions – such as – I'm not able to, I don't know how to...

These beliefs will stop us from achieving what we want in life. As we all look through life with a different lens, it is a well-known fact that people can be in the same situation/family and have a totally different experience. In order to understand this better let us look at the NLP Communication Model.

The NLP Communication Model

Every day we are bombarded by information coming into our brain. We take in 4 billion bits of information per second but, we are only aware of 2 billion bits. The way we take information in is through our senses – vision, taste, touch, smell, and hearing. In terms of visual processing, we can only cope with 1% of this information or else the brain would be overloaded.

When information comes in, we **FILTER** it in 3 ways.

Delete – as it does not catch our attention. We selectively pay attention to certain aspects of our experience and not others. We then overlook or omit others.

Distort – is where we put our own interpretation or understanding on it.

Generalise – is where we draw global conclusions on something based on one or two experiences.

Filters are based on our previous experiences and personality. (I will cover personality in a bonus chapter at the end of this book). What we end up with is our own stored **internal representation** of that experience.

There are many other filters that we use:

- Values
- Beliefs
- Language
- Meta Programs
- Attitudes
- Memories and time

These are found in the unconscious mind, and we may not be fully aware of them until we bring them into our conscious awareness.

Values – are high generalisations that describe what is important to you in life. I have covered this already.

Beliefs – are subjective ideas about what is true and not true for us, and the world that we live in. These are developed through our exposure in the world and modified by the perceptual filters of distortion, generalisation, and deletion. They act as the rule book in our lives as to what we can and cannot do.

Language – describes experiences, they are not the experience itself. Often, a person's language will influence their view of the world. For example, bilingual people frequently say they feel and behave differently when speaking another language compared to another.

Meta Programs – These are unconscious mental short cuts that we run in our minds which filter our experiences. There are 15 in total, but I will outline the top eight.

Meta Programs filter and store information in our mind. We filter and code information that is linked to our values and shape our personality – like a frame of mind or a pattern of thinking that lies above and beyond the actual words or content that is being said. Meta Programs are on a spectrum that people move up and down along a continuum.

They are useful as they give you a better understanding of how you and others think. They can be used in coaching, selling and interviewing/presentations, recruitment, advertising, and marketing. They can also help with conflict resolution. We learned from understanding personality that some people like sameness while others like difference. Knowing these programs that people run is useful in understanding how people operate in the world and make choices accordingly.

The way to establish someone's Meta Program is to ask them a question. I do a lot of this questioning when I am working with you during an intake session to find out how you operate within the world.

1. Motivational Direction Filter – involves a goal and is related to gains/winning (towards) or avoiding something such as deadlines, must do's and should do's (away from). Motivational Direction Filters is what will keep people tied to a job, as they like the security of a salary.

Question: What do you look for in your work?

Often a person who lacks confidence will have an away filter, i.e. I don't want to be, do or have X, Y or Z.

2. Frame of Reference Filter – internally referenced (i.e., they know when you have done a good job) or externally referenced (i.e., they need validation from others).

Question. How do you know when you have done a good job?

Often a person who lacks confidence will look for validation from an external source, i.e., they need to be told by their boss that they have done a good job.

3. Chunk Size Filter – this refers to what size of information they need - specific/detail or big picture or global view. (Some can be between the two).

Question. If we were doing a project together, how would you like me to give you feedback in detail or bullet points?

4. Action Filter – this is when someone is proactive or reactive.

Question. Do you wait for others to act, or do you prefer to be autonomous and move forward without much information? Do you act quickly, or do you need to analyse first?

For example, often those who lack confidence will not take the lead for fear of exposing themselves or making a mistake and being judged.

5. Stress Response Filter – how do you react; this can be disassociated (outside unemotional) detached showing no emotion. Or associated this is a thinking mode associated with feeling.

Question. Tell me about how you handled a difficult situation at work? (Will they have an emotional response or a thinking - report like response with no emotion).

6. Reason Filter – How does a person like to reason? Is there a continual search to find alternatives or is there a preference to establish procedures? In other words people will be either options driven or may prefer to follow procedures. People who like options will are motivated by opportunities and possibilities. People with a procedure's preference would like to follow set ways of working.

Question. How do you approach your daily work? Do you prefer to follow procedures or go with the flow?

7. Relationship Filter – Some people like sameness and others like difference. Some people will stay in the same job, relationship, home for all their life and others will change frequently as they get restless easy.

Question. How often do you change your job/car/house?

Often those who lack confidence will stay in jobs for a long time as they don't have the confidence to apply for jobs or go for an interview.

8. Convincer Representation Filter – how do we get convinced? Some people will make decisions quickly; they are 'automatic convincers' whereas some prefer to think it over for a while or sleep on it. These we refer to as 'number of times' type of people.

Question. How do you know that one of your colleagues is good at something?

Question. How often do you need to hear from people, or see performance before you become convinced about them?

It is important to recognise when communicating with others that most people are visual 50- 60%, followed by 30% who are auditory and the remainder being kinaesthetic or get a feeling.

Attitudes – are positive or negative evaluations of people, objects, events, activities, ideas, or just about anything at all. They are formed from our past as well as our present experiences. I will talk more about this in a later chapter.

Memories – of our life which can be positive or negative and how we store those in time and space which is unique to everyone.

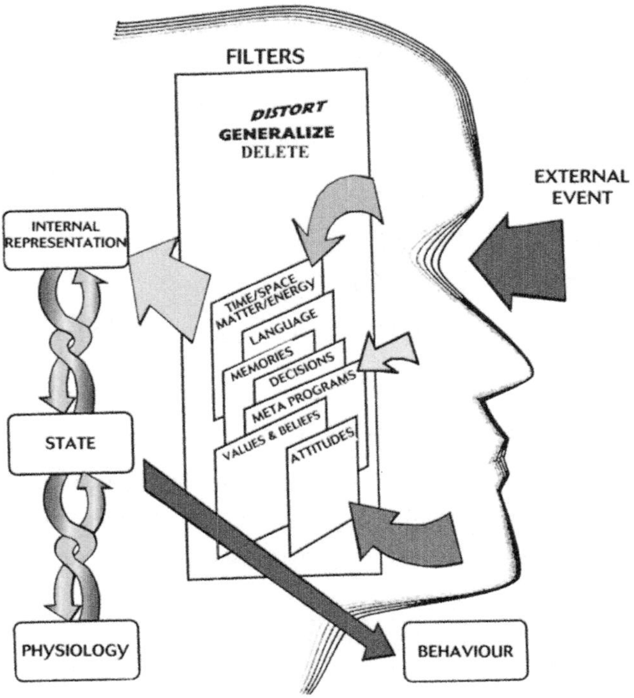

Figure 1: NLP Communication Model

All the above filters go to form someone's **Model of the World,** how they see it and how they operate within it. This forms their internal representation. This in turn will control our state. Our state is how we think and feel. Our state will then result in our outward behaviour. Thoughts will always come before feelings, this in turn will affect our behaviour and ultimately our results. This NLP model of communication in Figure 1 is one of the major themes that we use in NLP to make sense of the world in which we live. These themes give us confidence when communicating with other people as it gives us a framework in which to be able to respectfully challenge people's model of the world when they become stuck.

NLP Tool #1 - Physiology of Excellence

- ✓ If you want to change your behaviour, you can change your state.
- ✓ If you want to change your state, you can change your internal representation and your physiology.
- ✓ If you want to change your filters, you can change your projections.
- ✓ If you change your projections, you will change your external events.

State Control

Now that you are aware of the communication model and how it affects our state, you can choose to change your state at any point. We are in control of our mind and therefore our results.

NLP Tool #2- Changing Your State

If you want to change your perceptions and experiences, try experimenting with this exercise over the next few days.

Try out the different physiology of various positive states by thinking of situations when you are in a great positive state such as feeling motivated and confident, or calm and relaxed. Stand up, have a shake, or walk and change your physiology into that of a practised positive state that would be more useful to you. Adapt your posture, stance, breathing pattern, what you see or hear or what you are telling yourself and anything else that you need to replicate the physiology of that positive state. Stay with it for a while and notice what happens and how you feel differently. Now re-emerge yourself into what you were doing previously by keeping the positive physiology. Notice what is different.

Summary

In this chapter we looked at the NLP Communication Model. I outlined the filters that we use to enable us to cope with the information that is coming into our mind. Values and beliefs are two of these filters. We explored the meta programs that we run and how these are how we operate in the world. We finished the chapter with some NLP tools to help control your state so you can achieve better results.

CHAPTER 2

Growth Versus a Fixed Mindset

"Whether you think you can or you think you can't, you are right either way."

Henry Ford

Introduction

I lived my life in the shadows for 25 years as I allowed my beliefs to hold me back. I believed that I was not clever enough to BE a doctor. I thought that I had to settle for being a nurse. I didn't think I could write a book as I was dyslexic. I didn't think I could do a science-based degree as I didn't understand maths. I didn't think I could start a business as that was for other people and not me. I didn't think I would have a property portfolio or investments. Before I found NLP and personal development, I had a fixed mindset and didn't believe I could change. All my negative thinking kept me stuck and not taking action to achieve my hopes and dreams. Now you might be just like me and wanting to know HOW to break free of that and that's why I wrote this book.

Like you I always felt that I wanted more from my life. I believe that everyone has huge untapped potential inside them, you just need the key to unlock it. FEELING IS THE SECRET. The key that unlocked me was when I became a mother, I will talk more about this later in Part 2 -Mission.

Fixed Mindset

What is a fixed mindset?

According to psychologist Carol Dweck, "in a fixed mindset, people believe their base qualities, like their intelligence or talent, are simply fixed traits and they cannot grow. They believe that they were born with certain level of ability and are unable to improve that ability or talent."

I believed that because I was a 'C' student I could only be a nurse and not go to university. But this belief was installed in me by other people. I just chose to adopt that belief. That belief did not serve me and it's not serving you. If you have a belief that you can't BE, DO or HAVE something in your life, that belief is holding you back. We need to shift away from that.

Do you have the symptoms of a fixed mindset?

1. Believe intelligence and talent are static.
2. Avoid challenges to avoid failure.
3. Ignore feedback from others.
4. Feel threatened by the success of others.
5. Hide weaknesses so as not to be judged by others.

I want you to do this exercise NOW. It will get you started in making the shift.

Coaching Tool - Be, Do, Have, Activity

We are going to explore everything that you want to BE, DO or HAVE. This will assist you to set short, medium, and long-term goals.

Please devote ample ***thinking time*** to each stage highlighted below.

Step 1

Write down all the things that you want to BE, DO or HAVE.

Step 2

Write in one brief sentence why you want to BE, DO, or HAVE each item on your list. If you can't do this with any of them, cross them off your list.

Step 3

Decide the most important areas of your life – for example:

- Family
- Friends
- Career/Work
- Financial
- Health & Vitality
- Emotional well-being
- Social life
- Fun & recreation
- Physical environment (where and how you are living and your surroundings)
- Spiritual life

Add, change, or delete to include all the areas of life that are important to you. Define what success means to you in each of the life areas you have identified.

Step 4

Take each of your goals in turn and ask the question:

Will having, being or doing this thing improve the areas of my life that I deem are important? Give one mark for each ***Yes*** answer.

Step 5

For each of your goals, ask if it is right and fair to everyone in my sphere of influence and concern and if it will take you closer to your overall objective.

Step 6

Put your goals in order. Take your top 10 goals. These are the ones that you are going to work on first.

- Define your goals into 4 main groups:
    1. Ongoing goals needing daily input.
    2. Short-term goals to achieve within a week to a month.
    3. Medium-term goals that may take between a month and a year.
    4. Long-term goals that may take longer than a year.

Step 7

For each of the goals on the list, expand your ***WHY***. Explain to yourself fully why you want to have this goal and what it will mean to you. Write this down.

Step 8

Take each goal in turn and make two 'to do' lists for each to show:

- What are you prepared to do to achieve it?
- What will you need to do to achieve it?

Step 9

Make a list of:

- The people you need to work with.
- The people who can help you.
- The skills you might need to develop.
- The actions you need to take.
- What you need to learn.
- What you need to understand.

Step 10

Complete the rocking-chair test. Take yourself out into the future to age 82. Imagine a wonderful life you have designed for yourself. Visualise it. Fully associate with this and get into the feeling that you have already attained it.

Write down the story of your incredible life, the amazing things you've done, fantastic things you've seen, the people you have touched and the changes you have made in your own life.

Place your goals with their action points, within a timeframe. Put a start and finish date on them. Remember, a goal is a dream with a date.

Great job, you have acted and moved yourself into a GROWTH mindset.

Many people who have a fixed mindset lack confidence and remain in their safe place. I know as I was one of these people for many years. I now use my experiences to help entrepreneurs who are afraid to put themselves out there, get visible and find their voice.

Confidence

What is confidence? Simply put, confidence is the art of doing something successfully and repeatedly over time. When we do something for the first time it will feel scary and awkward. When I was a nurse, it was part of my role to deliver training. I tried every trick in the book to get out of it. I remember when I first started training in front of a large audience. It was frightening and I had to practice my content many times before I presented. I still felt all those feelings of 'fear' and my flight/fight response kicked in, fast heartbeat, sweaty hands, dry mouth. However, once I had delivered it, I felt happy in how it went and that gave me more confidence for the next time. I pushed myself into my stretch zone and I learned a new skill which over time became my comfort zone.

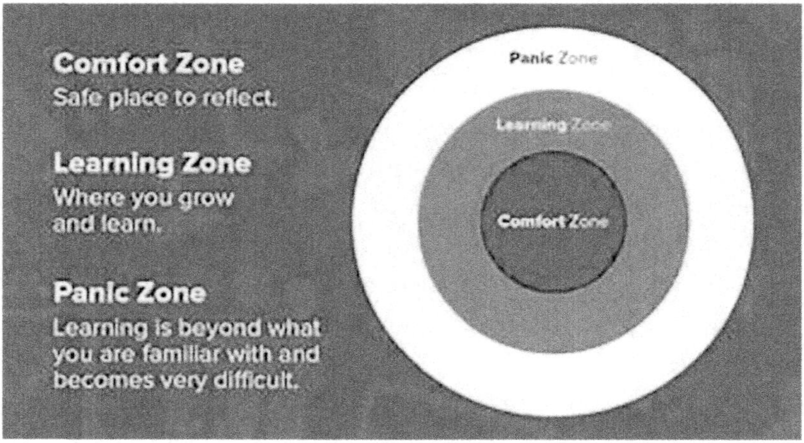

Figure 2: Zones of learning

If you go back to the NLP Communication Model in chapter one, confidence comes under one of the filters that we have. It is a belief (or not) in oneself, the conviction that one has the ability (or not) to meet life's challenges and to succeed—and the willingness (or not) to act accordingly. Being confident requires a realistic sense of one's capabilities and feeling secure in that knowledge. So where does lack of confidence come from? Well, as mentioned in the last chapter, it comes from our upbringing and experiences of being parented and this forms our thoughts and beliefs that we hold about ourselves. Some of these beliefs are conscious and many are unconscious and lie deep below the surface. The conscious thoughts are what we say to ourselves.

- I am not good/pretty/intelligent enough.
- I do not have enough experience to go for that job.
- I can't be X, Y, or Z.

We will talk more about this in the next chapter.

Before then let's explore what a growth mindset looks like.

Growth Mindset

A growth mindset simply means that people believe their intelligence and talents can be improved through effort and action. A growth mindset also recognises that setbacks are a necessary part of the learning process and allows people to bounce back by increasing motivational efforts.

Features of a growth mindset

1. Failure is an opportunity to grow.
2. I can learn to do anything I want.
3. Challenges help me to grow.
4. My effort and attitude determine my abilities.
5. There is no failure only feedback.
6. I like to try new things.
7. I am inspired by the success of others.

As I shared with you before I had many limiting beliefs but then I found Neuro Linguistic Programming and my life changed forever.

I got rid of all my negative emotions and limiting beliefs and changed my mindset.

I came out of the shadows and into the light. I found my voice.

I gained my degree in psychology, two master's degrees, one in therapeutic counselling and an MBA. I published 3 academic papers for my PhD. I wrote my first book (this is my second). I started up 6 businesses from scratch. I went to the top of my profession in nursing.

My mentor Kim Calvert has taught me that we must willingly give and graciously receive. I have always believed in this practice of giving back and helping others in life. I have volunteered for many years. Currently I volunteer on a board of Trustees for a homeless charity; it is something very close to my heart. I also volunteer as an Executive Coach in the NHS (National Health Service) Leadership Academy to help other nurses to progress in their career. At the time of writing this book I am reading the GO-Giver by Bob Burg and John David Mann. I would thoroughly recommend it. It gives us an important lesson about business, life and our time – our most valuable asset.

I don't list my accomplishments to brag but to show you the power of a growth mindset.

You just need to make the DECISION to change.

Here are my top tips for cultivating a growth mindset.

1. Practice and write out 10 things you are grateful for each day.
2. Acknowledge and embrace imperfection in yourself and in others.
3. Do something that scares you a little bit every day.
4. Face your challenges bravely.
5. Pay attention to your words and thoughts. Be careful what you tell yourself because you are always listening.
6. Stop seeking approval from others and trust your intuition.
7. Take a step deeper into authenticity, be real and be you.
8. Cultivate a sense of purpose and find your WHY in life.
9. Turn criticism around until you find its gift, there is no failure only feedback.
10. Value the journey over the result.
11. Learn from your mistakes and that of others, take the good and forget the rest.
12. Take risks and set your intention.
13. Be persistent and don't give up, keep moving forward.
14. Continuously learn and grow your awareness.
15. Have a positive attitude – what you give out will come back to you.
16. Be brave and step out of your comfort zone.

Summary

In this chapter we looked at what a fixed versus a growth mindset is, and how to recognise its features. We did the BE, DO and HAVE activity that helps you move from a fixed mindset to a growth mindset. We examined what the comfort zone looks like and how to move into your stretch zone. I shared my top tips on growing your confidence so you can move forward and go after your goals.

CHAPTER 3

Conscious Versus the Unconscious Mind

"Whatever we plant in our subconscious mind and nourish with repetition and emotion will one day become a reality."

Earl Nightingale

Introduction

Not everyone understands how the mind works and when you ask, most people to think of a picture of the mind and it will be a picture of the brain that pops into their head, as we all think in pictures. It can be a problem if we are unable to see this clearly.

The conscious mind involves all the things you are currently aware of and are thinking about. It is mainly how we process information that is coming into our mind from our senses. Think back to the NLP Communication Model. As mentioned previously in chapter one, our senses are what we see, hear, feel, touch, and taste.

The unconscious mind is a reservoir of feelings, thoughts, urges, and memories that are outside of our conscious awareness. Let's look at the difference between the conscious and unconscious mind.

Conscious Mind

I refer to the conscious mind as the GOAL SETTER; it is the thinking part of the mind. This is where we set all our intentions. The conscious mind can accept or reject what you plant there. Many people like you and me to achieve greater things in their life, but many people do not write down their goals. This is where many fail at the first hurdle. I have a daily habit of writing out both my personal and professional goal and I would encourage you to do the same. Let me explain why.

There was a famous study carried out by the Harvard MBA Business School between 1979 and 1989 amongst the students on the MBA graduate programme. They were asked the question, have you set clear written goals for your future and made plans to accomplish them? The results of that question were: only 3% had written goals and plans. 13% had goals but not in writing. When they did a follow up study 10 years later, the 3% that had written down their goals were earning 10 times as much as the other 97% combined. The 13% who had goals were earning twice as much as the bottom 84%. The 84% that did not set any goals were earning much lower income amounts. (Harvard MBA Business School Study).

Unconscious Mind

This alone is powerful, but we need to take goal setting a step further and plant it in the unconscious mind, as this part of the mind can only accept that which we plant there. The unconscious mind is like a fertile garden. We need to nurture it; this is how our thoughts become a reality, visualisation will help achieve this. My mentor Kim Calvert at Dynamite Lifestyle has as her strapline **"If you can see it in your mind, you will hold it in your hand".** Therefore, we need to move our goals into the subconscious mind – this is the GOAL GETTER. The unconscious mind is where the feelings lie, and we need to tap into the feeling if we want to get to the result. FEELING IS THE SECRET.

I attended her event in December 2021 and since then have been on my own personal journey of 'Thinking into Results'. It was Kim that introduced me to the concept of the 'paradigm.' I was not familiar with the word paradigm or the impact of it on my thinking even though I had been in the personal development world since 2009.

What is a Paradigm?

A paradigm is a multitude of habits that we have formed that hold us back. Everything that we think, feel and do has been imprinted on our subconscious. This is learned behaviour and we have repeated so many times it has become our default in how we respond to situations.

It was my paradigm that kept me stuck for 25 years.

This is how Bob Proctor defines the paradigm.

"Paradigm is a term used to describe a mass of information that is programmed into an individual's subconscious mind genetically at the moment of conception and then environmentally after birth. The paradigm is what structures a person's logic".

To put it in another way, paradigms are like mental messages that 'hang out' in our unconscious mind and these act as our saboteurs fighting against us in what we want to achieve. They are like the 'mind monkeys' that keep talking to us, stopping us from moving forward and achieving our goals. Paradigms control every move that we make.

Prior to studying with TIR, this was my understanding of the conscious and the unconscious mind. We are all familiar with the concept of the iceberg. We can thank Sigmund Freud (1856 - 1939), the well-known neurologist and founder of psychoanalysis for this image, as it was, he who came up with the image of the iceberg.

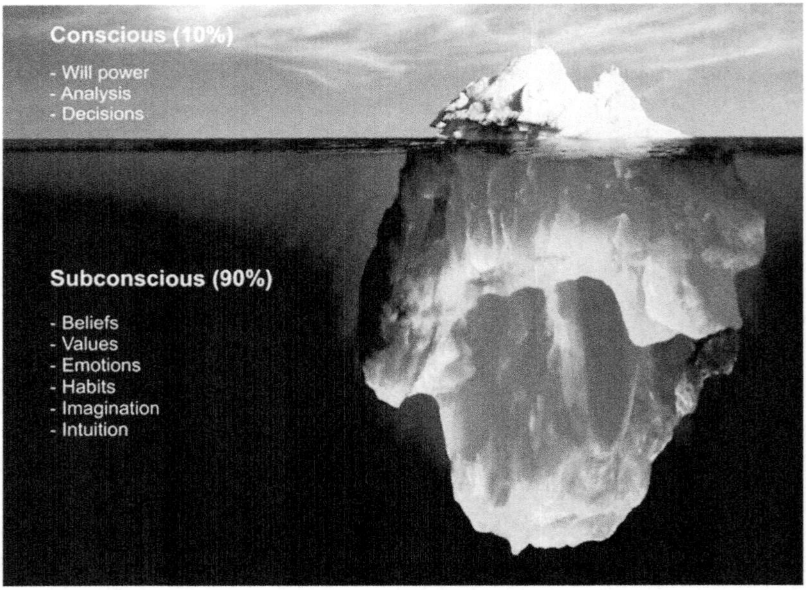

Figure 3: Conscious versus unconscious thoughts

According to Freud, the conscious mind or surface thoughts only account for 10% of all our thoughts, with 90% laying beneath the surface ingrained in our unconscious minds. This figure will vary depending on whom you study with.

I chose to adopt the teaching of the foremost leader in the field in personal development, Bob Proctor, may he rest in peace. He was in life my mentor's mentor, and he still is as he is to me, and many of you reading this book. Bob Proctor is the most well-known and respected expert in the field of personal development, and he suggests that the conscious mind only accounts for 3-5% and the unconscious 95-97% so we must work on the unconscious mind if we are to achieve results. But it is also important to recognise that success is 95% mindset and 5% strategy. Many entrepreneurs including myself, get this wrong and spend 95% on the strategy and only 5% on the mindset and wonder why they are not progressing. When I worked on my mindset everything changed.

If you don't change your mindset, nothing will change, you will remain stuck in your life and your business. Both Bob and Kim have taught me about the power of awareness and moving from fear into faith. They also introduced me to the 'Stick Person.' This simple but wonderful image has changed my thinking and it will help you understand how you too can 'Think into Results'.

Let me introduce you to the 'Stick Person' as explained to me by Kim Calvert, my mentor.

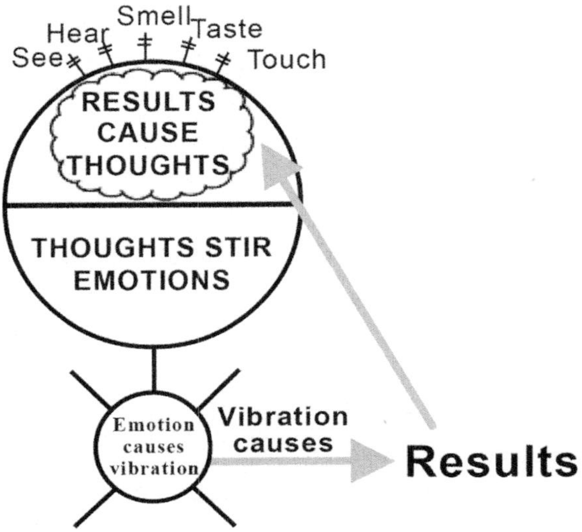

Figure 4: The Stick Person

In short, our thoughts become our actions. When I work with you, I work on changing your values and beliefs, and loosening up your model of the world and moving you from a place of negativity into positivity. It's all about our attitude. These all lie deep in the unconscious mind. I am a very positive person; I am the eternal optimist, and my glass is always half full. I surround myself with positive people who lift me up and leave me in a good vibration. I would advise you to do the same.

Attitude

I believe to be successful you have got to adopt an attitude of gratitude. One of my daily habits is to write down 10 things that I am grateful for every day. This is followed by writing out my personal and professional goal as I have already mentioned and then my paradigm shift. I meditate for 10 – 15 minutes before I start my day. I will always set my intention for the day ahead and this puts me in a good vibration for the day. I make a decision that today is going to be a GREAT day.

Attitude is a combination of thoughts, feelings, and actions. By doing this daily practice I keep moving forward in achieving my goals.

During my life and work I come across many people that have a negative attitude towards life. Their glass is always half empty and they feel that the world is against them. They live in a victim state and don't take responsibility for their actions. They are at the effect side of life rather than at cause. My job as an NLP coach is to get them shifting from the effect side of life over to the cause side of life. This shift will help them move forward.

Whatever you plant in your unconscious mind will grow, it does not have the ability to reject what is implanted there. It can't tell the difference between reality and fantasy. That's why it is so important to use your imagination and visualise what you want and then get into the feeling of it to bring it into reality.

Case Study

Melanie was a nurse. She came to me as she was frustrated that she had applied for many jobs and had been turned down. She could not understand the reason behind this. Her confidence was low, and she wanted me to coach her to a successful outcome. Having taken a history, I soon discovered that Melanie had a limiting belief about herself that was holding her back. She believed that she could not ask for clarification on a question at an interview, as the panel were the ones in authority, and she had to be submissive (this belief came from her schooling). She believed that she could not question the panel; as a result, she could not answer the question correctly and thus gave the wrong answers.

We worked together in role play in building the confidence to seek clarification on questions she was not sure about. I loosened her model of the world by gently challenging her beliefs and reframing her thoughts. We then focused on what it would look like to have been offered the job; what she would hear, feel and see and we anchored this feeling so she could be in a more resourceful state. Melanie achieved a job promotion after her second interview.

Five Exercises to Build on Your Self Confidence

1. List 20 skills you have.
2. List 5 times in your life where you have overcome adversity.
3. List 5 people you have helped.
4. List 10 things that you love about yourself.
5. List 5 achievements of which you are proud.

Communication is an art, and it is important that we understand both ourselves, and other people to fully be able to put ourselves in another person's shoes. This will give us a competitive edge in life and enhance our emotional intelligence in dealing with people. Confidence is something that you need to work on and if we are not confident YET you can learn to be. But we must move out of our comfort zone and be willing to be stretched as in the case of Melanie. If you believe this, you can achieve great things.

Summary

We covered a lot in this chapter, we looked at the conscious mind and the unconscious mind. I explained about what a paradigm is and how these can hold you back from achieving your goals. We touched on attitude and how our thoughts and feelings influence our actions and behaviours. We talked about confidence, and I gave you some of my top tips on growing your confidence as this goes hand-in-glove with growing your mindset.

PART TWO:

Mission

CHAPTER 4

A Worthy Goal

"If your WHY doesn't make you cry, then it is not BIG enough."

Unknown

Introduction

I had been thinking about how to spend more time with my family and still earn money. One thought led to another - I am a qualified Montessori Teacher, I am a Children's Nurse, I know about childcare and education. All these thoughts led me to an idea.

I decided that I was going to set up my own Montessori Day Nursery and be with my family. From my own experience of being a mother, I knew that there was a gap in the market for good childcare provision. I took a leap in faith, sold the family home, and with my husband's blessing bought a home that would double up as a business.

I did not know the how, I just had a burning desire to be with my children – to be able to attend their Christmas plays, go on school trips, and not have to worry any more about being late for school drop off and pick-ups. I would be my own boss and I would be FREE. I was terrified, but I pushed through the FEAR as the pull factor was so strong. I had my WHY. I stayed focussed on the result and I moved forward with conviction.

There were so many unknowns at the time.

- I did not know if we would get planning permission to convert the residential home into a business.
- I did not know how I was going to get the money to convert the downstairs floor into a nursery.
- I did not know if I was going to be able to get the staff.
- I did not know how to do the policies and procedures that would satisfy the local authority or the Ofsted inspectors.
- I did not know if I would get any parents who would want to attend my nursery.

All I knew was that I was going to make this a success no matter what it took. I set my intention, that I was going to up open the nursery in March 2004. I set this goal and I was going to go after it, but I had never done anything like it before. I drew on something deep within myself that I did not know was possible. I grew hugely during the process. This goal really stretched me out of my comfort zone into my stretch zone and at times to my panic zone. I still lacked confidence in myself and felt fearful, but I did it anyway as my desire was so strong, it pulled me forward.

Types of Goals

I did not know back then but this was a 'C' type goal. I only learned this when I started studying with Kim Calvert, my mindset coach. I will talk more about this in the next part of this book.

'A' type goals, are goals that we know we can achieve. 'B' type goals, are goals that will stretch us a little bit out of our comfort zone. 'C' type goals are what we really want. I REALLY wanted to be with my children. I would do whatever it took.

'A' Type Goal What you know you can do

- Present Results

B Type Goal What you think you can do

- You make a plan and work towards it

'C' Type Goal Fantasy

- What I Want

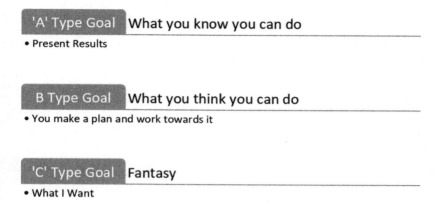

Figure 5: A, B and C Type Goals

Happy Faces Montessori Nursery was a 'C' type goal born out of a worthy idea driven by a desire to be with my children.

I opened my first nursery on time and on budget within six months. All the resources came to me at the right time, the money, the staff, the clients. I just put it out to the universe and manifested a successful outcome. I then opened my second – a baby unit in 2007.

Going after your 'C' type goal takes courage, it will need to be backed up by a burning desire and a belief that you can succeed.

I have now been in business for the past 13 years. I started with a bricks and mortar business and have gone on to set up five other businesses. I never thought as a shy, introverted person that I could succeed but when your WHY is big enough you will find a way.

It is important to say that I did not find NLP until 2009.

I faced many challenges in the first five years of my business and admit that at one point they nearly broke me physically and emotionally. But I refuse to live in past. This book is about empowerment, and I only focus on the positive in my life. I take the learning and forget the rest.

I wish I had known then what I know now as I would have saved myself a lot of hardship. But everything happens for a reason. All experiences make us the person we are today.

How we think, is how we behave. Be careful what you think about as YOU are listening. Only think positive thoughts.

NLP Tool #3 - Neurological Levels of Thinking

This is based on the work of Robert Dilts who was an anthropologist. This is a great tool for exploring the reason behind what we do. It is like peeling back the layers of an onion. It provides an insight as to what level a person is operating at so I can work with you helping you achieve a positive outcome or goal.

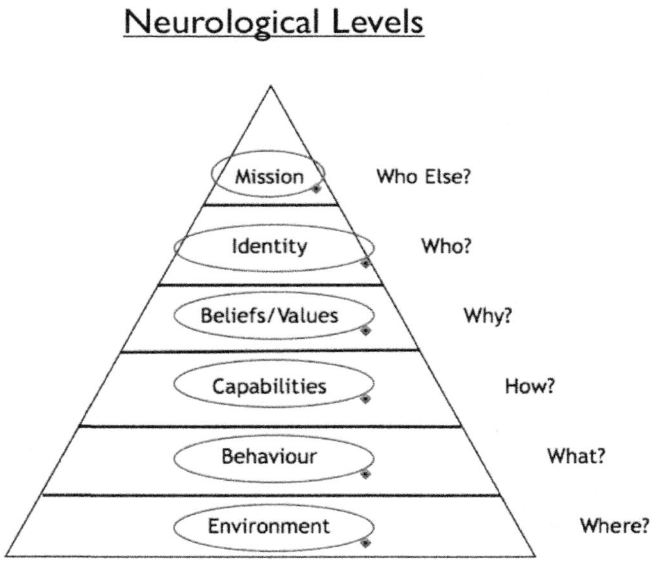

Figure 6: Neurological Levels

Environment

The environment is what and who is around us that will have influence over us and the choices we make. This is what we react to. I had the support and belief of my husband that I would succeed in my wanting to open a nursery.

When I work with you at this level, I ask questions like Where? What? and With Whom?

Behaviour

Behaviour is what you do and say in certain environments. It is an external expression of the self. But people are not their behaviours, so if someone is angry, sad, difficult this is not the person. But it is human nature to label people as their behaviour. In NLP we say accept the person and change the behaviour. I took on the behaviour of a successful businesswoman and acted as if I was that person. We have all heard of the phase fake it until you make it. In my new world of thinking I prefer to use the words 'acting as if' you have already achieved what you have set out to do.

Skills and Capabilities

This is how we perceive and direct our actions. It is how we do what we do – from physical, emotional, and psychological perspectives. These are the strategies we use by applying our cognitive abilities. Capability involves proficiency over behaviour and is a higher-level processing in the brain's cortex. I knew I had the skills and ability to care for children at a high level, as I was a children's nurse and health visitor for the under-fives. I knew much about health, nutrition, child development and early years education as I trained as a Montessori Teacher when I had my second child. I had a natural empathy and compassion for caring as a mother and care giver. I had all the tools and resources I needed to be successful in my business. But this must be backed up with belief.

Values and Beliefs

We have previously spoken about these in Part 1, but to repeat, values and beliefs are fundamental judgements and evaluations we hold about ourselves, others, and the world around us. Neurological beliefs are associated with the limbic system and hypothalamus, the more primitive part of the brain. Beliefs can be both empowering and limiting. These are at the core of motivation. They relate to the question, "Why?"

My WHY was big enough to drive me forward to success.

Identity

This is the sense of who we are as an individual, it is our special way of being in the world even from infancy. Neurologically, identity is associated with our nervous system but may involve the reticular formation deep within the brain. Our perception of our identity organises our beliefs, capabilities, and behaviours. Transformation of identity can have a huge, almost instantaneous effect on our physiology. With every small success that I had, I grew in faith and belief. I got the planning permission despite some resistance, I got the money so I could employ the builder, I got the policies and procedures written (with a little help from a specialist in the field), I got the staff, and I then got the parents to come. I had become the successful business owner through my journey into results. This came about because I acted 'as if' I already was that person.

Purpose

This involves your connection to something that goes beyond yourself, it is our mission or purpose in life.

My purpose in life is my FAMILY.

When I work with you, and you want to make changes in your life I will always start with your values as these are the corner-stones of our decision making and action planning.

Summary

In this chapter we looked at how life circumstances can drive our decision making. How having a desire will set us into action. The importance of setting a 'C' type goal and acting as if you have already achieved it. We finished with looking at NLP Tool #3, The Neurological Levels of Understanding and emphasised that by placing your mission at the top of the hierarchy, this is what will drive you forward to achieve your goal.

CHAPTER 5

Desire

"To succeed in your mission, you must have single-minded devotion to your goal".

A.P. J. Abdul Kalam

Introduction

I had a burning desire to be with my children, this was my motivation to move me towards my goal, I was laser focussed on my mission. My thoughts became my feelings, my feelings became my actions.

At the time of purchasing the property I was still working part-time as a nurse and had employed an au pair to help with the children. I have always had au pairs to help me with my children as I don't have any of my own family living in the UK.

I used to ring up every day to find out how my daughter was. On this particular day I could hear my daughter crying in the background. I asked the au pair why she was crying and why she wasn't comforting her. She said she wouldn't eat her food. In that moment, I made decision. I was going to give up work, my daughter needed me in her life to give her that comfort. I became fully focused noy only on my daughter but my three sons and my goal of opening the nursery.

According to Napoleon Hill in his book, *Think and Grow Rich*, He states:

> *"Every person who wins in any undertaking must be willing to burn his ships and cut all sources of retreat. Only by doing can one be sure of maintaining that state of mind known as a burning desire to win, essential to success".*

I had faith that I would be successful in my mission that my nursery would succeed. Faith is the opposite of fear, and if I am honest, I was still fearful but my desire to be with my children kept me focused on the result. Many, of you reading this book might be thinking that you need confidence and belief to make these decisions and the answer is YES you do. But it was faith and desire that pulled me forward. If I can do it so, can YOU.

As at that time I was not a confident person, all I had was a burning desire that helped me push through the fear. With every success I built my confidence. When I went to the Town Hall to defend my planning application, I was scared. I had to stand up and answer questions from the panel as to why and what advantage this nursery would provide to the community.

I felt those old familiar feelings surging up inside me. I was experiencing fear. I had done this strategy so often in my mind that it was automatic.

Fear

When we are fearful or stressed, the body produces the stress hormone called cortisol. Cortisol is an energising hormone which increases the level of blood sugar. It is released when we experience a threat and the body's response is fight, flight or freeze. This is great in the short term to provide energy to react quickly, but in the long term it can be bad for the immune system. Excess release of cortisol over a long period of time can lead to increased risk of strokes and heart attacks. When blood sugar levels are raised, it can lead to inflammation of artery walls. This damage can cause the immune system to respond, leading to a build-up of fatty deposits which can block the arteries. If some of this build up breaks away and is released into the bloodstream, then it can block smaller arteries that lead into your brain or heart.

There are also psychological effects of high cortisol levels. Stress can limit our ability to think clearly. When we are stressed our 'amygdala' is responsible for labelling information coming into the brain. If this is perceived as threatening it limits activity in the cerebral cortex, the part of our brain that allows us to think strategically. This reduces our ability to make decisions, be sociable and take on new ideas and information. It means that we cannot function like we normally would and as a result, you may act in a way that you might later regret.

I was nervous and I did stammer a bit, but I got my point across as I had a burning desire. This was what motivated me to move into my stretch zone. But I did it and I WON and so will you, you just need to make that decision.

Now some of you may still be uncomfortable in finding your voice like I used to be. But confidence is like a muscle you must keep exercising it and you will GROW.

I lived with lack of confidence for many years before I broke free. I ran the script in my head so often and it was a well-rehearsed pattern of behaviour. This was how I lived my life for 25 years.

Strategies

We all have strategies for everything that we do in our life; from getting up in the morning to going to bed at night, there will be many strategies that we run through in our mind throughout our day. We have a strategy for every activity that we do in our daily lives whether it be decision making, motivation, parenting, eating or wealth creation.

Many of you, like my old self, will have a strategy for fear. It will always begin with a thought, followed by a feeling, which will in turn result in our behaviour. I didn't know back then about this material. But somehow, I was able to go past the FEAR and do what I needed to do, and I succeeded in getting a positive outcome as I had the desire.

Since I have found NLP, my life has changed so much, and this is now what I use to help you get what you desire in your life.

I remove strategies that don't serve them and install a new more helpful strategy.

NLP Tool #4 - The Keys to an Achievable Outcome

When I work with you, I will ask you to reflect on this question - What Do You Want? How is it possible that you do not have what you want now?

I will then walk you through this process and this set of questions:

Is the goal stated in the positive?

1. What specifically do you want?
   Many of us want something to stop so we will say, "I do not want to be fearful any longer" or "I don't want to be struggling for money anymore." It is so important that you state your intention positively. In NLP we call this working towards something rather than away from. So, I would reframe the intention or goal. For example, you might say, "I want to be able to speak with confidence" or "I want to have more money."

Specify the present situation.

2. Where are you now? – this question allows exploration and gathering a baseline assessment of where you are at right now. The reality of your situation.

Specify the outcome.

3. What will you see, hear, feel, be saying to yourself, etc. when you have it? I get you to associate into the result, so you are emotionally involved in the result.
   - Act 'as if' now – I get you to visualise that you have already achieved a positive outcome.
   - Make it compelling – making it as realistic as possible. I can tell when this is achieved you will have a big smile on your face.
   - Insert it in the future – give it a date of when you have achieved your goal.

Specify evidence procedure.

4. How will you know when you have it?
5. Is it congruently desirable?
6. What will this outcome get for you or allow you to do?
7. Is it self-initiated and self-maintained?
8. Is it only for you? Or does it affect others?
9. Is it appropriately contextualised?
10. Where, when, how, and with who do you want it?
11. What resources are needed?
12. What do you have now, and what do you need to get your outcome?
13. Have you ever had or done this before?
14. Do you know anyone who has?
15. Can you act as if you have it now?
16. Is it ecological?
17. For what purpose do you want it?
18. What will you gain or lose if you have it?
19. What will happen if you get it?
20. What won't happen if you get it?
21. What will happen if you don't get it?
22. What won't happen if you don't get it?

Outcome and goals

There are certain aspects that need to be considered when goal setting. These include:

- Stated in positive terms.
- Initiated by you.
- Specific, sensory-based description of the outcome/goal and the steps.

- Ecological.
- More than one way to get the outcome or achieve the goal.
- Does the outcome/goal increase choice?
- Keeps the positive by-products of the present situation.
- Achievable and realistic.

For you to have a positive outcome, goal setting needs to have three essential components.

1. An aim or end in mind.
2. Aim relates to direction.
3. End relates to outcome.

I overcame my anxiety and fear as I had a MISSION and a purpose. I felt the fear and I did it anyway because the desire was bigger than the fear.

I was completely out of my comfort zone; remember, I was still living in the shadows. I didn't find NLP until 2009 (5 years after setting up my first business). I didn't know what I know now. I stepped into my power, and I claimed it for my children, and I was successful.

You can too, if you step into your power. We all have untapped resources hidden inside of us.

If you are stepping out of your comfort zone and feeling a little anxious like I was when I was presenting to the panel, you can try visualisation to help you I just went to my happy place and visualised the birth of my first son and the feeling of elation that I had at that time. I didn't know at the time I did this that it was an NLP technique for state control.

NLP Tool # 5 – Changing State

1. Think of a time when you felt really, really, happy. I want you to see what you saw, feel what you felt and listen to what you heard.
2. I want you to really get in touch with the feelings, thoughts and sounds that you are experiencing.
3. Then I want you to intensify those feelings by turning up the dial so that you can feel the sensation of happiness, success or joy that goes with that emotion.
4. Just enjoy that new altered state for a few minutes which will immediately calm and bring you to a more positive state.

Practising this on a regular basis will alter your state and you can then anchor this state and use it as a resource for success to help to achieve your desired outcome.

Anchoring - What is anchoring?

The process by which any sensory representation, internal or external (the stimulus), gets connected, linked to, and triggers a subsequent string of representations and responses (the response). It is often known as the use of any sensory stimulus to condition responses. Anchors can be naturally occurring or set up deliberately.

When I work with you, I get you into a positive state and then I anchor that state to enable you to access it at any time to get you out of the state of anxiety, worry or doubt. Anchoring is based on the work of classical conditioning by experimental neurologist, psychologist and physiologist Ivan Pavlov and his experiments on dogs in the 1970s. A stimulus response can happen in any of the senses.

- An image/scene - Visual
- A piece of music - Auditory
- An external feeling - Kinaesthetic
- An internal feeling - Kinaesthetic
- A certain smell - Olfactory
- A particular taste - Gustatory

We can all associate back into a time and place that we experienced any one of the above events. I have a particular smell of a flower called 'Sweet William' and this makes me always associate this smell with my granny, who I had much love for.

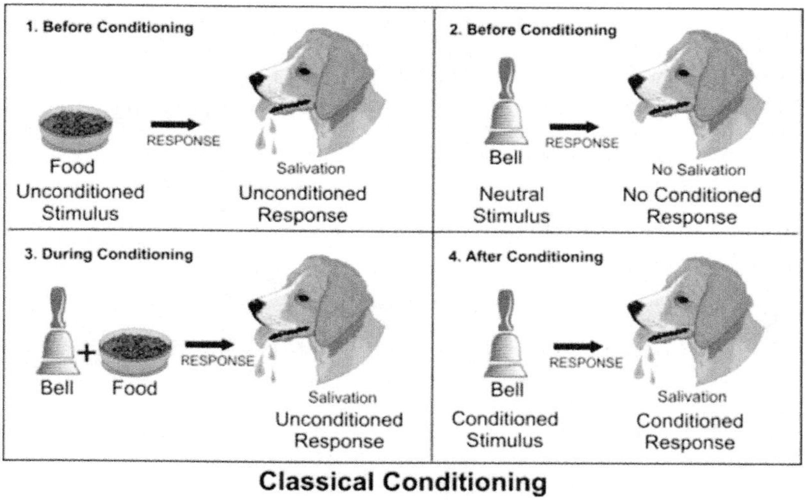

Figure 7: Classical Conditioning

At times I will stack anchors with you. This is where we put several resource anchors on top of one another to make it as compelling as possible. I can chain anchors; for example, when I need to get you from a highly emotional state like overwhelm to a calm state. I would take you from one step to another as the leap from overwhelm to calmness is too great. I can also collapse anchors where I get rid of unwanted states. To achieve this, we would 'fire' two different anchors simultaneously. This causes a mix of anchors resulting in neutralising the feelings.

Summary

In this chapter we explored desire. Many people have desires or wants in life, but they don't go after them. They are held back by negative feelings like worry and doubt. This leads to fear, and people remain stuck. Confidence is the way forward and helps us take steps forward in faith. Fear is the opposite to faith. In this chapter,

I gave you some tools to help you get into a resourceful state and help you to move forward and make decisions that may be holding you back from having that which you desire.

Confidence is a belief that we hold about ourselves. In order to grow our confidence, we just need to practice it. Most people wait to find their confidence before doing something, but the key is just to act; every little step you take will build you up more and more. I have developed a resource to help you if you need a confidence boost.

GIFT

I want to thank you so much for reading my book this far. I am so happy and grateful that you have spend this time with me, and I want to show you, my appreciation.

I want you to grow like me in confidence and achieve all that you desire in life as you deserve it. Please scan the QR code so you can download my gift to you.

SCAN ME

FREE Copy of *10 Steps to Improve Confidence and Grow Your Self Esteem.*

CHAPTER 6

Persistence

"Nothing in the world can take the place of persistence. Talent will not. Nothing is more common than unsuccessful people with talent. Genius will not. Unrewarded genius is almost a proverb. Education will not. The world is full of educated derelicts. Persistence and determination alone are Omnipotent. The slogan 'press on' has solved and always will solve the problem of the human race"

Calvin Coolidge

Introduction

There will be times when you want to give up on your goal and your dreams especially when you have doubt, worry and feelings of fear creep in -- and thoughts of failure surround you.

I had those too as that is the paradigm talking to you trying to pull you back down into your safe place. There will be good times and there will be bad times, that is the law of rhythm. I had many challenges and obstacles put before me during the start-up of my first nursery and at times I didn't know if I was strong enough to make it through. But persistence is the key to success, and you only fail when you give up.

Challenges

I had multiple staff issues. I learned quickly from making mistakes and I course corrected. I had to bring in a uniform policy as one of my female staff used to come into work inappropriately dressed. One hot day she decided to come to work in 'hot pants' and a very low top which was very distracting especially for father's and not something that I wanted reflected in my professional brand.

I supported staff with personal issues from homelessness, immigration, and substance misuse problems. I mentored and coached them all to get the right help and support.

I had a mother who assaulted me because I refused to remove a child with special needs from the nursery who had bitten her child. So, I had to ask her to leave the nursery.

I had another mother who decided to sue me as her child had accidentally fallen from the slide and broken his arm. This was a particular sadness as I showed this mother much kindness; she had problems paying her fees and I gave her time and exemptions to meet her payments. One day her car had broken down and she and her child could not get home. I drove her home myself so that she and her child could be safe. I believe in willingly giving and graciously receiving. However, this graciousness was not returned to me. This mother was most persistent in making my life difficult and ruining the reputation of the nursery.

She made a complaint to Ofsted in the UK; this is the Office for Standards in Education. I had inspectors come down and investigate my processes. As child safety is of paramount importance to me, I could demonstrate this in my documentation. My risk assessments, safety plans and staff ratios were well within acceptable limits. The mother then made a complaint to the health and safety executive. I had more inspectors come down and they spent four hours in my nursery going through all my policies and procedures. Again, I was vindicated as all my processes were in place.

She finally decided to take a civil suit against me as she was looking for monetary compensation. My insurance company decided to settle out of court despite my protests, as I wanted to protect my reputation.

But despite all these challenges, I remained persistent. I knew deep down that what I was providing was an excellent service. I had received an 'outstanding' judgement from the local authority. When you are persistent you will become a leader in your industry. Bob Proctor states that 'Whatever you conceive and believe, through persistence you must conceive' I agree. Decide right now to be one of those people who is persistent. It is for this reason I called my business Believe to Achieve Coaching.

If you are in alignment with your WHY and are persistent in that path, you will be able to handle the challenges along the way. The road may have twists and turns, the plan may change, but the destination remains the same. To me that destination was spending time with my children. This is my highest value in life and what drives me forward despite the challenges I faced. However, I had not anticipated what was to come into my life at that stage.

Turning Point

A week before Christmas 2007 I was covering at the baby unit as the manager was off sick. I was observing the staff and noticed how one member of the staff was interacting with a child. I felt she was neglectful to the child's needs. I was so concerned about her lack of compassion and empathy that I asked her to leave my employment. She had information about the nursery that I was not aware of, and she blew the whistle to Office for Standards in Education (Ofsted). A significant safeguarding event had occurred, and all 10 members of staff covered it up. A child who was on an induction morning had been left outside in the garden as the staff had forgotten he was there. This event was covered up by all 10 members of staff on the instruction of the manager. Within a few days I had Ofsted come down to the nursery and investigate the incident. During the investigation it was uncovered that policies and procedures had not been followed. The risk assessments had not been kept updated and other documentation were missing. This was a direct reflection on my nursery and the safety of a child. I was served notice to correct all the failures of the nursery manager. I had put my trust in other people, and I had been badly let down. I ended up having to dismiss three of my employees over this incident. This was a very low point in my life and in my business. I made the decision that I would have to sell the business. I felt morally bound to phone the mother of that child and inform her of what had happened to her child. She was so kind to me and thanked me for my honesty.

At that time, I was functioning at a much lower values level in life. I allowed my thinking to affect my feelings and my behaviour. I regretfully did not have the tools or resources to persist through this major life event.

This was before I found NLP.

My top value in life is family and caring for children and this had been breached at such a deep level in my thinking. I felt broken. I couldn't eat, sleep or function my whole world was shattered. I was barely able to function in life and that was when

I made the decision to sell both of my nurseries and take some time out to heal. My values level thinking was rock bottom at this stage in my life and it had affected my decision making.
Where do you sit in your values level thinking?

Values Levels Thinking

This is based on the work of Tad James. According to him there are three elements to a values level. First, there is the container (the nervous system) in which the values are held. Then there is the environment, in which the person lives and then the behaviour. Values Level Thinking are numbered 1 - 7 and in NLP we give them colours. Levels 2, 4, 6 and 8 are the sacrificial 'We/ Us' values. Whilst 1, 3, 5 and 7 are the selfish 'Me' values. When coaching my clients, it is useful to know at what values level they are functioning at.

Beige – Survival "Me" type values

Values Level 1

This values level is associated with the 4 F's – Feeding, Fighting, Fleeing and F***ing

- Behaviour is instinctive and automatic.
- Functioning at the essence of human survival.
- Uses deep brain programs and senses.
- Distinct self is barely awakened.
- Lives much as other animals but slightly higher level.
- Minimal impact on environment.

Purple – A Clan "Us" type values

Values Level 2

Mentally associated with this values level is "can my people survive"? Family is important such as found in 'mafia' or 'gang culture'. There will be rituals and sacrifices involved. All for one and one for all.

- Obey desires of mystical spirit being.
- Show allegiance to elders, custom, clan.
- Preserve sacred places, objects, rituals.
- Bond together to endure and find safety.
- Live in an enchanted, magical village.
- Seek humanity with nature's power.

Red – My Powerful "Self" type values

Values Level 3

The mindset will be one of a Win: Lose situation; wants to win at any cost, ego- centric. Buy or Die attitude, kill the competition, no constraints, no conscience. Lives in the now mentality. Feelings associated with this values level are anger, rage, grief, disgust.

- Every man for himself type of attitude.
- Express self, to hell with others.
- Escape domination by others or nature.
- Avoid shame, feel no guilt, get respect.
- Gratify impulses and senses immediately.
- Fight to gain control at any cost.
- Not constrained by consequences.

Blue – A Righteous "Us" type values

Values Level 4

What is bigger than me, a guiding singular force, bigger than you. Associated with regulations and standardisation, a search for the truth, sense of what is right and wrong. Feelings associated with this values level is fear, anger, and guilt as it is associated with judgement of self by others. Puts off satisfaction with a mentality of I will get rewarded later but you must suffer now. Example working in a job that you hate for the reward of a pension later in life.

- Finding a meaning and purpose in life.
- Sacrifice self to the way for the Truth.
- Bring order, stability, and future reward.
- Control impulsivity through guilt.
- Enforce principles of rightful living.
- Divine plans put people in proper places.

Orange – My Strategic "Self" type values

Values Level 5

Associated with a Win: Win mentality; I want the power to control my own destiny and have an impact on other people. Wants things quicker and faster; give me the good life attitude. Mentors and coaches fall into this values level. Values Level 5 hate Values Level 6's.

- If it isn't broke - then break it and make it even better.
- Strive for autonomy independence.
- Seek out the 'good life' and abundance.

- Progress through the best solutions.
- Enhance living for many through technology.
- Play to win and enjoy competition.

Green – Our Communitarian "Us" type values

Values Level 6

Values Level 6 is all about the love; no-one is in charge we are all on the same level. It senses feelings deeply. They are driven by guilt, hurt and depression. They are aware of the energy a Values Level 7 person has but want to be functioning at a Values Level 8.

- Liberate humans from greed and dogma.
- Explore the inner beings of self/others.
- Promote a sense of community and unity.
- Share society's resources among all.
- Reach decisions through consensus.
- Refresh spirituality and bring harmony.

Yellow – An Integrated "Self" type values

Values Level 7

Those with this values level will be doing something at a world level. Focus is on efficiency and getting results. They are self-motivated, arrogant, time is valuable to them. They have no need to prove anything. Love complexity. They love 'doing' and acting.

- Accept the inevitable of nature's flows.
- Focus on functionality, competencies.
- Find natural mix of conflicting 'truths'.

- Self-interest without harm to others.
- Experiences fullness of living on Earth.
- Demands flexibility and open systems.

Turquoise – A Holistic "Us" type values

Values Level 8

These people will be working on a planetary level. They will have a synergy of life and be interconnected. They will be reworking Values Level 2 but on a much higher level.

- Blending, harmonising, strong collective.
- Focus on the good of all living things.
- Expanded use of human brain/mind tools.
- Self is part of larger, conscious whole.
- Global networking seen as routine.
- Acts for minimalist living so less is more.

Our values must be in alignment with who we are and who we want to be. When I sold the nurseries, I did it as was no longer in alignment with my goal in serving other families or indeed my own. I was in conflict. Conflict will block us from moving forward in achieving what we want in our lives and who we want to serve.

When I work with you there may also be some conflict in what you want to do, what you want and where you want to go. You may self-sabotage yourselves by stopping and starting and jumping from one thing to another. I will talk more about our saboteurs in a bonus chapter.

For me I have always been a risk taker' when I decide to do something, I go all in. I knew that I would rise again, and I did. I love change and have always gone against the crowd. For example,

I have never gone into a pension, I prefer to invest that money in personal development.

I have always been a risk taker and I think this is because I get bored easily. I really admire people who stay in their job for many years. Since I found NLP, I just became a different person. I never worry about job security and love the freedom of being self-employed and being my own boss.

I have gained much more awareness about the mind since my training as a master practitioner of NLP back in 2010. Through my continuous journey into personal development, I now have a growth mindset and I have a positive mental attitude. I continue to grow my level of awareness through mentoring and coaching. One of my mentors Kim Calvert has taught me how to use our Higher Mental Faculties (HMF) to succeed in life and business and I would like to share them with you.

What are the HMFs?

If we go back to the diagram in chapter three, I introduced the well-recognised image of the iceberg. What we see above the water is the conscious mind, and we now know that this only accounts for 5-10% of our results depending on the teaching you follow. So, let's explore these Higher Mental Faculties a bit more deeply as even these are not used to their full capacity. The 6 HMFs are:

1. Memory
2. Reason
3. Will
4. Intuition
5. Imagination
6. Perception

Let's take each one and talk about how they can serve you in increasing your results and behaviour.

Memory

Memory is different than your memories which are found in the unconscious mind. I have always thought that I had a terrible memory as that was because I have dyslexia and my short-term memory is awful. I can't even remember something from five minutes ago. But I am challenging that negative belief and trying to expand my memory as I am learning there are many ways to help improve memory. One thing that kept me in a job for 15 years was that I didn't want to go for an interview. I believed that I didn't have the confidence to succeed. I used the excuse that I couldn't remember the questions and therefore could not give an answer. This belief held me back for many years. I have now found fun ways to remember things and to use memory to my advantage. Like for the 6 HMFs, I apply a mnemonic device to the first letters of the six words and I use "MR WIIP" to remember "Memory" all the way to "Perception". This allows me to think of all the letters and I can access what they stand for. It has been so useful in helping me remember things. I am happy for you to take that one as my gift to you. I now use this in most things in my life; it's like a key that unlocks the information for me to enter the information that is stored in my brain.

Reason

I believe reason is what holds us back from achieving what we want to achieve in life. We want to stay employed as we have a regular income coming in, it gives us security. Being self-employed is dangerous. We should make sure we get a well-paid job and pay into a pension, and we will be OK. But this is not true.

The definition of reason is as follows:

> *"Reason is the capacity of consciously applying logic by drawing conclusions from new or existing information, with the aim of seeking the truth".*

I used to reason with myself all the time about why I couldn't do what I wanted to do in life. But the problem was I continuously based my decisions on old information that was not true, they were all based on false beliefs. I was making decisions based on what other people had told me about me. You might be doing the same thing as me and you need to STOP, and think, is this a truth or is it a lie? We all know that F.E.A.R stands for False Evidence Appearing Real and it's so true. You need to rewrite your own story and don't let other people hold you back from achieving your goals, desires, or wishes for a better life.

Will

The WILL is key to success. It's about making a conscious choice and sticking to it come what may, just as I did despite the challenges that I faced within my business. It's about mastering any negative beliefs that may hold you back from what you want. People who have a strong desire will progress; they are able to leave worry and doubt behind them and step into faith.

The WILL allows us to stay focused on one thing and not be distracted by other shiny objects. Many people will self-sabotage by moving from one thing to another and never completing anything. There are so many things that demand our attention today so having a strong WILL is key to your success.

Intuition

Many of us will refer to our intuition as our gut feeling. I have always had very strong intuition; I think this is from my background as a nurse. I had to make quick decisions as in many cases my patient's life would depend on it. I had to learn to trust my intuition, and it has always served me well. If I don't feel aligned with something, then I will remove myself from it. It's that little voice in our head that tells us something is not quite right, or something feels off. It is always important to follow it.

Imagination

Our imagination allows us to create something out of nothing, like I did with my two nurseries.

I have always been good at having ideas and bringing these ideas into thoughts. Many people have ideas but don't act on these, which is a lost opportunity.

When I sold the nursery in 2008, we invested in a property portfolio to have passive income coming into our lives. I took a year off; I was in a position where I was able to do this. I spent a whole year thinking about what I wanted to do and where I wanted to go in my life. This is when I entered the world of personal development. I will go into this in the next part of my book. As this is when my life changed forever.

The mind is a marvellous machine, and we can have anything that we want. We just need to decide and go after it.

Perception

Perception is how we organise, identify, and interpret sensory information that comes into our mind and how we understand and interpret that. Most people have the perception that you should not leave a well-paid government job like nursing as its secure and you have a job for life.

I am a risk taker and love a challenge. Successful people take risks. I have always gone against the grain. When I worked for the National Health Service, as mentioned previously, I decided not to pay into a pension as it would tie me down and keep me in a job. That's what made it easy for me to leave my job and start my first business.

We are conditioned from an early age that we should get a good education, go to university, work hard and get a good job and then you will be secure for life. If you work hard, you will succeed and be happy.

Joan had a perception that she was not able to study at a higher level as she was dyslexic, and she wouldn't be able to understand the technology. She perceived her dyslexia as a barrier to what she wanted to achieve in her life, and she was filled with worry and doubt. But she persisted in her endeavor and was rewarded.

Case Study

Joan has dyslexia she hadn't studied for a long time; she was fearful of how she could learn on a computer as most of the learning would be carried out remotely. She was worried about going back to learn and how she would cope with the challenges of her dyslexia. She was held back by a limiting belief that she had about herself. Working with Joan I was able to shift her thinking into more empowering beliefs and she successfully qualified as a reflexologist.

Identifying your limiting beliefs

Everyone has some limiting beliefs; this is normal especially when you are doing something that you have never done before. A limiting belief has the following features:

1. A belief that encapsulates a general viewpoint that you have about yourself, others, or the world in which you live.
2. A belief that is dogmatic; that is, it's something that you don't think to challenge, or you regard as always true.
3. A belief that in some respects is not helping you to achieve outcomes you'd like or is reinforcing your low opinion of yourself.

Coaching Exercise

Changing Limiting Beliefs to Empowering Beliefs

Limiting Belief	**Empowering Belief**
My success is limited by my education and experience	My motivation and enthusiasm for life will attract new opportunities
I don't believe anyone will pay me for my services/business	My creativity and desire are all it takes to attract paying customers to me effortlessly
I don't know how to run a business	I can learn how to run a business; my resources include X, Y and Z

A specific limiting belief could be:

I won't pass this exam

The underlying limiting beliefs associated with this self-critical thought could be:

- I'm stupid, or
- I always fail, or
- I never get what I want

Limiting Beliefs & Your Past

Beliefs are learned from experience and from the messages you are given by others.

If you're continually told by someone important to you that:

- You lack certain qualities or have certain negative characteristics,
- You won't achieve very much,
- You shouldn't do certain things,

Then you may start to believe those things.

This can happen when you're a child because your parents or other primary caregivers, family, teachers, and friends are the nucleus of people that know you. And when you're young, you begin learning from others before forming your own opinions, as you do when you get older.

It can also happen when you're an adult, if you receive negative messages or experience negative events.

If those close to you give you positive messages, such as:

- You are worthwhile,
- You are loved,
- You are entitled to have your own opinions,

Then these are likely to be helpful to your self-esteem.
Sometimes however, amongst the positive messages, it's the negative messages that you remember.

Understanding and Explaining Limiting Beliefs

Another way of helping you to gain control over your limiting beliefs is to:

1. Write down what your limiting belief is.
2. Identify how they came to be something you believed, whether through being told by those closest to you, through personal experiences, or through other reasons.
3. Instead, write a constructive statement about what you're doing to help yourself think more positively.

For example:

Step 1 – My Limiting Belief:

I often feel or think that I am worthless.

Step 2 – Brief Explanation:

I feel this because when I was younger, my parents seldom complimented me and often criticised me.

Step 3 – Constructive Statement:

I now realise that I do have positive qualities and I'm making efforts to change my belief patterns.

The problem with Limiting Beliefs

The thing to realise with limiting beliefs is that what starts out as a protective device becomes a destructive habit. It will hold you back from achieving the success you want and deserve. What you get is what you focus on. Author and coach, Tony Robins, states that *'energy flows where you focus goes'*. Some people put all their energy in the wrong place. So, when we ask ourselves questions like:

> Why am I not confident to speak in public?
>
> Why am I so stupid, why don't I understand this?
>
> Am I fooling myself in thinking I can run my own business?

The brain will search for the answer and find evidence for it. The brain is always listening in to what you tell it. You become your thoughts.

Instead, I want you to turn these questions around. Ask yourself:

> How can I become more loveable and successful?
>
> How can I learn and make this work?
>
> I am passionate about business; what do I need to do (or believe first) to get paying clients?

And then the unconscious mind will get to work on solving that issue. The unconscious mind is the goal getting and it works tirelessly in achieving that answer even when you are sleeping. Do you believe that you have the resources inside you to overcome these limiting beliefs?

Below is a technique that I use with clients who lack confidence.

NLP Tool #5 - SWISH Technique – Confidence Builder

What is a SWISH?

This is a useful pattern of interrupting habits and replacing them with new, positively constructed ones. Habits become strongly ingrained through repetition. SWISH uses repetition of the new sub modality pattern to extinguish the old habit by swapping the sub modalities from one context to another. Sub modalities are the subsets of modalities (visual, auditory, kinaesthetic, gustatory and olfactory) that form our internal representations and understanding. This technique uses rehearsal to intensify the compelling nature of the new, more helpful habit.

In NLP we use SWISH when wanting to change any undesired behaviour by replacing a behaviour or habit that you no longer want with something that serves you better.

In case of a lack of confidence, I use a Kinaesthetic SWISH. Representing both the unwanted behaviour and the desired behaviour as pairs of shoes using the principle of swapping sub modalities.

There are 4 steps to the SWISH

Step 1

- Bring up the bad feeling attached to the behaviour or habit. This can be something like getting nervous when you speak and feeling anxiety. Send the feelings down to your feet and imagine that feeling to be a pair of shoes.
- Describe the shoes in full Visual, Auditory, Kinaesthetic, Olfactory and Gustatory (VAKOG) terms. Make them as unpleasant as possible. (For example, choose dirty trainers or high heels/pointed toes - could be tight, as in one size too small, hurting skin, pinching, scruffy, horrible colour, etc.).

Sub modalities help make the feeling, picture, smell, taste more intense.

Such as - warm/cold, tight/loose, dirty/clean, good/bad smell, good/bad taste etc.

Use the sub modalities and your language to make that feeling as real and uncomfortable as possible. When I work with you, I use my visual acuity to calibrate/read that the feeling you are experiencing to ensure it is intense and unwanted).

Step out of them and put the shoes to one side

BREAK STATE - distract yourself by asking a question - what did you have for breakfast?

Step 2

- How would you like to feel instead – comfortable/relaxed?
- Create that desired behaviour as a different pair of shoes
- Put them on and feel how they are in VAKOG terms

This time you may choose a nice pair of comfy slippers; they are warm and comfy, and soft on their skin. This makes you smile just thinking about the feel of them on their feet.

Step out of them and put them to one side

BREAK STATE - Ask yourself another question - what are the last 4 digits of your telephone number?

Step 3

- Put back on the negative pair of shoes
- When you are ready remove them, either pop them off, throw them in the bin, or burn them
- Experience the feeling of getting rid of them

Step 4

- Immediately replace the old shoes with your preferred pair of shoes
- Experience that feeling
- Practice walking about in your new slippers
- How different is that for you?

This technique needs to be repeated to embed the new behaviour because old behaviours sometimes can be hard to break. If I find the behaviour is not changing for you, then I use another exercise called 'Neurological Levels' to completely disrupt and change your thought behaviour (I covered this in an earlier chapter).

NOTE: SWISH technique can be used in both kinaesthetic and visual senses, in the case of confidence I chose the former as confidence is a feeling.

In general, your driven by whether something feels good or bad for you. You move away from negative feelings or emotions. It's what causes you to act or not take act.

When I work with you, I find out whether you are a 'towards' person or 'away from' person. I then use this in my coaching to get the best out of you.

The secret of success it that people form a habit of success and do what failures don't like to do or are afraid to do. The problem is that so many of us from an early age just like me were told, "You can't."

You can't be a doctor because you are a 'C' student.

You can't do Physics and Chemistry because you are a girl.

You can't read and can't spell because you are dyslexic.

You can't speak in public.

Can't is a word that paralyses progress and creativity.
I choose that I CAN. Reaching the goal is not success; success is moving towards the goal.

Summary

We covered much in this chapter about persistence. I started with sharing some of the obstacles that I had to overcome. I gave you the process of how to set an achievable outcome. I explained about values level thinking and how these can be 'Me' or 'Us' driven. I outlined the Higher Mental Faculties (HMF) and how they can assist you in your thinking and creating the results that you desire. I concluded the chapter in talking about limiting beliefs and shared a tool about how you can change them into empowering beliefs, along with another NLP SWISH tool to build your confidence.

PART THREE:

Moves

"To Improve is to change, to be prefect is to change often."

Winston Churchill

CHAPTER 7

Personal Development

Introduction

The events that I had experienced in the nursery had left its impact on me and my health. I had felt let down by both staff and parents. It had really affected my confidence in how I had allowed events to get on top of me and that was the reason I decided to sell up to be more available to my family and look after my health. I had lost faith in people and was feeling very let down by the circumstances that I found myself in. I was in victim mode, and I didn't like it; I felt disempowered. The feelings of *fear, hurt* and *sadness* had reawakened all those feelings from childhood. I needed to take a whole year out to recover from my experiences.

I realised that I had to change as my confidence was holding me back from who I wanted to be and who I wanted to become. I felt that I had huge untapped potential if I could rid myself of *fear.* I found the answer in personal development and Neuro Linguistic Programming (NLP).

In this chapter we will explore 3 aspects needed to move you forward in life and in your business: Personal development, Mentorship and Coaching and Mastermind Accountability Groups.

But what shifted the needle for me was NLP. In this chapter I will explain what NLP is and how it can help you also through its application. I'll also cover the benefits of NLP coaching and how it changed my life and how it can help address some of the issues in your life that may be holding you back. I'll offer how NLP can be applied to different challenges that you face in life to help you move forward into a more empowered you.

Personal Development

When I started training as an NLP practitioner, I also decided to sign up with the Coaching Academy as a protégé student in the same year of 2009. Being a protégé student means that I have lifetime access to all their coaching programs which include:

- Personal Performance
- Business
- Continued Professional Development (CPD)
- Corporate and Executive
- Youth Impact
- NLP

Despite having set up two businesses, I still had a lack of confidence and would do anything to avoid any situation where I had to speak in front of people or read out loud. I would use all the excuses to get out of being visible or putting myself out there for fear of being judged. The experiences of my school days had left its mark on me.

I still had some negative emotions around fear, shame and hurt from my past and I knew that I needed to address this. I was constantly trying to prove to myself that I wasn't stupid as my teacher had labelled me all those years ago.

I had always sought a deeper understanding of myself and had a fascination with how other people operated within the world and what made them function at a deeper level. I decided to start my degree in psychology in 2007. This was while I was planning the opening of my second nursery along with training to be an Early Years Professional at Greenwich University. I somehow also managed to fit in being an Inspector with the Independent Schools Inspectorate (ISI) and being an Assessor for the Montessori Evaluation and Accreditation Board (MEAB). When I look back, I wonder how I did all that on top of my commitments as a mother of four young children. But I have a fantastic husband who helped with the kids. I don't think I could have done it without him.

It was whilst I was studying for my degree with the Open University in Psychology that I found out that I was dyslexic. It was a huge relief to know that I wasn't stupid; it was just that my brain functioned differently to other people. I now see my dyslexic brain as my superpower and making me the creative person that I am today.

This was like an awakening. I found out that I had a love for learning. Even with my dyslexia, I did not allow it to hold me back. I went on to obtain my master's degree in Therapeutic Counselling. I had a belief that I couldn't do a science-based degree as it involved much math's and statistics. However, I achieved my psychology degree in 2011. I was also studying simultaneously for my master's degree which I achieved the year before in 2010. I then went on to gain a second MBA in 2017 and went on to study for my PhD. I don't say this to brag; I was a 'C' student with dyslexia, but I didn't allow this to stop me from what I wanted. If I can do it so, can you. You just need to decide. If you want something bad enough, you will just go after it.

What is NLP?

NLP stands for Neuro Linguistic Programming (NLP). It can be incorporated into all areas of your world and help make improvements in your daily life. The main areas being:

- Health
- Relationships
- Education and Training
- Business and Finances
- Sport and Fitness
- Lifestyle and Leisure

I will outline what NLP is and how the principles and techniques can be applied in all the different areas of your life. NLP gives us more choices in our life and opens new possibilities.

As part of my approach, I offer a free breakthrough session to my clients who want to get to know me more and learn how I work. It gives an opportunity to see if we would like to work together on a longer-term basis. Mary, who is in one of my mastermind groups, reached out to me. I use open questions to help my clients find their own solution to the problem.

Sample questions:

1. What's working well?
2. What makes it work well?
3. What is the driving force that makes it work well?
4. What does your ideal life look like?
5. What is not quite right yet?
6. What tools or resources do you need?

Case Study

Mary had been procrastinating over her business for some time and was wasting much time in not being able to move forward or gain clarity and direction. By using my approach and drilling down, I was able to help her seek the clarity that she needed. She got her 'a-ha' moment. She moved from being stuck to unstuck, she then became a client of mine.

NLP is a way of changing someone's thoughts and behaviours to help achieve their desired outcomes.

NLP comes from a mixture of disciplines brought together.

N = Neuro/neurology – is the study of the mind or nervous system, how we think and our physiology.

L = Linguistics – is the study of language, how we use it and how it affects us.

P = Programming - is the sequence of our actions, how we motivate ourselves to achieve our goals.

NEURO

The nervous system refers to our brain which is a physical thing whereas our mind is a concept and relates to how we think and the physiology through which the experience is processed. It is how we store and use memories and how we represent the world to ourselves through our senses of which we have five.

Sight
Hearing
Touch
Smell
Taste

Linguistic

The language and other non-verbal communication systems through which our representations are coded, ordered and given meaning in our brain, including:

- Pictures
- Sounds
- Feelings
- Tastes
- Smells
- Words or self-talk

Programming

This is how we put our representations and language together to produce a set of coded instructions. The results create the patterns that we run in our lives, and the outcomes of these patterns.

For example, if we tell ourselves that we are terrible at public speaking, we will do everything possible to avoid this situation. We may have had a significant event that took place in our life that led us to a limiting belief or negative decision we made 'that I can't speak in public' and then we replay that message to ourselves in our brain repeatedly and that becomes our belief.

In other words, NLP is how we use language of the mind to consistently achieve (or not achieve) our specific and desired result.

Understanding NLP

There are three legs to NLP and the seat is what holds NLP together.

First leg - know your outcome; we covered this in a previous chapter.

Second leg - be aware of what your senses are telling you. Use your sensory acuity; this is the ability to read you through your facial expressions and micro movements, skin colour changes. In my interactions with you, this is what I use to calibrate or read what's going on for you. I build and maintain rapport by matching and mirroring. Matching is when I make the same gestures as you, if you take a drink, I take a drink. Mirroring is making the opposite movement to what you make such as if you raise your left hand, I will raise my right hand. Once I have gained rapport with you, I start to pace but not in an obvious way, it must be with good intention in getting you to follow my movements, that's when we are truly in rapport. All this is done at an unconscious level.

Third leg - be flexible I like to observe what's going on inside you. Is what I am doing getting you nearer to your goal/outcome. If not, I change my approach.

All of this is linked with the presuppositions of NLP which is the seat that holds NLP together. I will cover in the next section.

As an NLP coach I show genuine interest in you, I am curious and look at the world from your perspective. I will listen out for your predicates -- these are the words that you are using. Are the predicates visual, auditory, kinesthetic? I will try and match on four different levels - non-verbal, voice level, language level, and at the level of beliefs and values. NLP is an art form that can bring about life changing results if you take responsibility for your actions and are willing to change. In order to change you must be willing to take responsibility for your actions.

There are many themes in NLP, I have covered some of them already in Part 1 of this book such as the NLP communication model and the conscious versus the unconscious mind. In this part of the book, I want to focus on two further themes, Cause and Effect and Perception is Projection.

Cause and Effect

If we are to take control of our life, we need to be at 'cause', this is where we get results. What do I mean by this? Well, it means that we take responsibility for our actions or our inactions. This gives us a sense of empowerment. In NLP we always aim to be at 'cause' for the decisions we make. If we have made a mistake, we hold our hands up and admit that we were wrong and we will work to put it right. If you are at the 'effect' side of life that is a difficult place to be. These people will blame others for their shortcomings and their mistakes. They feel that are not in control of their lives. This means that they are powerless to change unless they change their perception. Some people will go through their whole life at the 'effect' side of the equation and never achieve their potential.

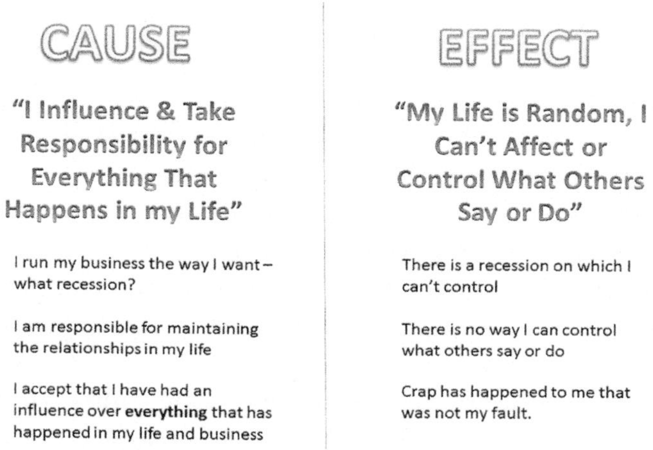

CAUSE
"I Influence & Take Responsibility for Everything That Happens in my Life"
I run my business the way I want – what recession?
I am responsible for maintaining the relationships in my life
I accept that I have had an influence over everything that has happened in my life and business
EFFECT
"My Life is Random, I Can't Affect or Control What Others Say or Do"
There is a recession on which I can't control
There is no way I can control what others say or do
Crap has happened to me that was not my fault.

Figure 8: Cause and Effect Equation

Perception is Projection

I am sure that you have noticed or admired a quality in somebody else and may even have said, "I wish I was more like that person." Or sometimes we may feel that someone has got you totally wrong and you're not sure as to the rationale behind their decision. I remember when I used to collect my children from school. All the parents would be huddled together chatting and laughing and I just stood on the side-lines. That was where I felt comfortable, as I am a natural introvert. Many parents used to think that I was not a friendly person, but the reality is I am quite shy, and I don't readily go up to people and speak to them. People's perception of me was that I was unapproachable and standoffish. This is far from the truth; I am a very friendly person but prefer to have interactions one-on-one.

It could be that a stranger has given you positive feedback by commenting that you seem like a confident person because you are going 'live' all over social media. These are all examples of how we are perceived by others. In NLP we call this "Perception is Projection." We aren't always consciously aware of it but it's happening constantly.

Yes, I do go live on social media, and I can still be an introvert and be a confident person. If you're just like me, you just need to have a belief in yourself. I am now a confident person I have learned by repetition and from failing forward. I want to encourage you that you can do the same you just have to make the DECISION and act.

If you spot something in somebody else it means that it is within you, because for you to recognise something in someone else, whether it be good or bad we must have it within ourselves first. In other words what we recognise outside ourselves is what we are inside; otherwise, how would we know what it was?

So, what you see outside you is really you. Everything you see, hear, and feel from the outside coming in, is understood, and explained within.

I now live my life as to how I want to be perceived and act 'as if' it's already here.

The Presuppositions of NLP

These are a set of beliefs that if we act 'as if' then they are true. It is a mindset that if you apply them, they will improve your life, they will help you in all areas of your life, including:

- Improving rapport by increasing understanding
- Reducing judgement against your own values
- Enabling you to see another person's point of view
- Increasing flexibility

As you read the below beliefs, which ones seem to resonate with you already?

Which ones of these are more difficult for you to accept?

What would it be like to 'Act as If' you believed them?

How might you think/behave differently if you did?

Which one could help you take a different perspective?

I have adopted the presuppositions of NLP; I abide by them and mirror them in all the interactions that I make. So, what are they?

1. **Respect** for the other person's model of the world.

This means that we all have a different view of the world which will differ to those that we work with or encounter in our lives. We all have different values and beliefs depending on our culture, religion, upbringing, parenting, schooling, peers, and media influences to name but a few. It is disrespectful to push your values and beliefs on others and it is not worth upsetting people. Sometimes we must agree to disagree on things that we do not see eye-to-eye on.

2. Behaviour and change are to be evaluated in terms of context, and **Ecology.**

When I work with you it is important to always check with you the consequences, results or impact of any change that occurs to you, others, society, and the planet now and in the future across all contexts. i.e., home, career, lifestyle. The way we check for ecology is to ask the following questions:

- What will happen if you do achieve X?
- What will happen if you don't achieve X?
- Who will be affected?

For example, if I had a woman who was lacking in confidence, and she came to me to increase her confidence, how would that affect her relationship? Would an increase in confidence put it under threat or make it stronger?

3. Resistance in a client is a **sign** of lack of rapport.

I recognise in my work that there are no resistant clients, only inflexible communicators. Effective communicators accept and utilise all communication presented to them. I change my language to be able to communicate on the same level as you, so we are speaking the same language so to speak.

4. **People** are not their behaviours. People are not angry, sad or hurtful people they have these behaviours but something underneath is driving that behaviour.

Accept the person and change the behaviour:

5. **Everyone** is doing the best they can with the resources that they have available to them. We all have a history and will have experienced different life events that make us who we are today.

Behaviour is geared for adaptation, and present behaviour is the best choice available. Every behaviour is motivated by a positive intent (even negative behaviour).

Some people do not have many resources available to them as they may not have had positive role models or experiences in their life, such as absent parents, or parents who were not protective, or were addicted to drugs or alcohol.

This is about forgiveness:

6. **Calibrate** on behaviour: The most important information about a person is that person's behaviour.

I read the person and flex my behaviour, to stay in rapport.

7. **The** map is not the **Territory**

The words we use are not the event or the item they represent. People will have a different meaning for the same word. Although the words we use to describe an event are chosen to represent the event, the words themselves are not the actual event itself. We create our own reality based on our past experiences, beliefs, and memories. NLP is the art of changing our map to create more changes.

8. **You** are in charge of your mind, and therefore your results. We must accept responsibility for our actions so we are at cause, if we blame other people we will never succeed in life or in business.

Who is driving the bus? Who's in charge?

9. People have all the **Resources** they need to succeed and to achieve their desired outcomes.

There are no unresourceful people only unresourceful states.

10. All procedures should increase **Wholeness.**

11. There is no failure only **Feedback.**

If a person is not successful in something, this does not mean they have failed. They have not succeeded, YET. They can take the learning and do it a different way next time. If what you are doing isn't getting you the results you want, do something different.

12. The meaning of communication is the **Response** you get.

We are taught that by clearly communicating our thoughts and feelings through words, another person should understand our meaning. But they will respond to what they think you said. You can determine how effectively you are communicating by the response you get from the other person you are communicating with. In addition, when you accept this presupposition, you can take 100% responsibility for all your communication.

13. The **Law** of requisite variety.

The system/person with the most flexibility of behaviour will control the system. When things aren't going your way, keep course correcting until you hit the target.

14. All procedures should be **Designed** to increase choice.

Becoming aware and gaining specialised knowledge and skills has been the cornerstone to my success. This is known as the law of compensation.

You will be paid in accordance with:

1. The need for what you do,
2. Your ability to do it, and
3. The difficulty in replacing you.

In 2010 I went on to study as a master practitioner in NLP. This took my skills to a higher level in NLP, Timeline Therapy and Hypnotherapy.

As part of this training, I underwent timeline therapy to rid myself of all negative emotions. I found this to be life changing. It is a very powerful technique that can free you from any previous negative experiences. The main experiences being, *Anger, Hurt, Shame, Fear*, and *Guilt.*

During my training as a counsellor, I had to undergo my own therapy for 4 years. I found therapy to be a very painful process of going into my past. I have to say, for me, it was not hugely beneficial and always left me feeling sad. It did not help me; but what did help me break free from my past was Timeline Therapy. Timeline Therapy is content free meaning that you do not talk about the past and you do not speak about any past negative experiences. If a person becomes emotional during the procedure, I take them out of it straight away, to keep them safe.

What NLP can do for you:

Neuro Linguistic Programming coaching provides the tools and techniques to help you:

- Read people better
- Manage your state (feelings and thoughts) more consistency
- Understand people's motivations
- Use language to improve your communication
- Break bad habits
- Visualise your future
- Get rid of anchors that make you feel bad
- Create anchors that make you feel good
- Change limiting beliefs
- Solve conflicts within yourself and with others
- Overcome and eliminate fears and phobias

- Stop behaviours that are no longer serving you
- Plan goals and achieve your outcomes

Coaching Exercise

How to Shift Your Self-Talk.

Let us use the example of someone wanting to gain more confidence in going live on social media. Put the emphasis on the bold letters and see how that affects your state.

I **SHOULD** start going live on social media
I **HAVE TO** start going live on social media
I **NEED TO** start going live on social media
I **COULD** start going live on social media
I **CAN** start going live on social media
I **WANT TO** start going live on social media
I am **GOING TO** start going live on social media
I **CAN'T WAIT** to start going live on social media
I **AM** starting to go live on social media

Act 'as if' the statements are true for you. Adjust your physiology and tone of voice as you would if the statement were true. See how different sentences shift your thinking and your state.

NLP Application

There are many ways in which NLP can be used in how to improve your life.

- Personal Performance - career, confidence, health, and fitness
- Relationships

- Business
- Education and Training

There are many tools and interventions that are applied in NLP, and I have tried to cover the main themes in this book.

- The NLP Communication Model
- Cause and Effect
- The Presuppositions
- The principles for achieving a positive outcome
- Rapport
- Reframing

Summary

In this chapter we looked at what NLP is and reviewed the 3 pillars of NLP, cause, effect, and perception is projection. We outlined the presuppositions of NLP and the application of NLP and what it can do for you.

CHAPTER 8

Mentoring and Coaching

"The delicate balance of mentoring someone is not creating them in your own image but giving them the opportunity to create themselves".

Steven Spielberg

Introduction

As a nurse I have always understood the concept of mentoring and I have always loved mentoring students in my career. I guess I just like seeing people develop and be the best that they can be.

But I didn't really understand the concept of coaching; I always thought it was related to the sports industry.

When I sold my nurseries that is when I started my journey into coaching. I had some money to invest due to selling my businesses and I knew that I wanted to help people. I had already started my journey into personal development and coaching just seemed to be a good fit.

I therefore decided to sign up with the Coaching Academy here in the UK and I went all in as a protégé student. This meant that I had access to all six of their diplomas and would have lifetime access to all their courses which would keep me professionally up to date. As mentioned previously, I started my journey as a coach in 2009 and gained my first diploma in personal performance coaching the following year. I have been coaching ever since.

The Difference between Coaching, Counselling, Mentoring and Consulting

There is a clear distinction between coaching, consulting, mentoring and counselling/therapy. Although I have been trained and am qualified in all four of these disciplines, I keep professional boundaries between all four in my work life.

As a coach I know when I am not operating within my professional competency and refer onto a counsellor if you are in distress or in need of therapy and then I resume coaching thereafter. Even though I am a qualified counsellor and can use my counselling skills to help you, I stay within my remit as a coach. Counselling delves into your past helping you to make your present better. Whereas coaching looks at the present, to improve the future. It is important that coaches like me recognise and stay within their professional competencies. I have had some clients come to me for coaching with past emotional distress, and sometimes that only becomes evident during the coaching relationship. I am able to know the difference and signpost to you on to someone else.

Therapy versus Coaching

The main points of counselling are as follows.

- Counselling/Therapy is about working with a patient who is unwell in their mind or thoughts.
- Therapy focuses on asking the question WHY?
- It takes for granted that emotions are a sign that something is wrong and therefore to be avoided.
- Generally, works with the person's past and the traumatic events and seeks healing of those events.
- If the person is suitably qualified, they can diagnose the emotional distress or mental illness and address the condition.
- It is centred on the doctor-patient relationship where the doctor has the solution, and the patient is the passive recipient. Carried out through conversation, it encourages the patient to talk about their feelings and thereby resolve their past pain. The focus is on reliving pain and to get rid of it.
- Is about fixing the person by understanding and fixing their past.
- The doctor/therapist targets a diagnosis for the patient and then puts forth his training in diagnosis and treatment of disease and then offers a path to healing.
- In most psychotherapy, the patient's progress is time consuming and can be difficult and traumatic for the individual opening old wounds and feelings.
- Focuses on the person being broken and needing to be fixed.

I found this to be true in my experience of therapy. I would often be in tears in a session and did not find it therapeutic at all, in fact quite the opposite.

Therapy often relies on the Diagnostic and Statistical Manual to diagnose pathology and operates on a medical model. There are many types of counselling/therapy to choose from including Person Centred, Cognitive Behavioral Therapy (CBT), Gestalt and Psychodynamic approach or integrative which is the approach that I am qualified in and use all of those listed.

As an NLP master practitioner during my training, I had a procedure carried out on me known as Timeline Therapy which is 'content free' – this means that you don't talk about your past traumas, or your feelings, and you get the solution without being emerges in the pain. This is the technique that changed my life forever.

I was able to get rid of all negative emotions. I no longer have inappropriate sadness, anger, hurt, shame, guilt, or fear. It is important to acknowledge the word inappropriate as it is appropriate to feel sadness if someone has died in your life for example.

Whereas coaching involves

Coaching is a collaborative experience where me as the coach works with you.

The coach asks the questions HOW, WHAT, and WHAT IF? I avoid the WHY questions as it assumes that you have done something wrong and can be associated with blame. It just gets reasons and not results. Coaching assumes that emotions are natural and looks for the intention and purpose for the expression of those emotions. I am interested in your present and I work to help you create a better future. I help you to discover the processes which prevents you from the achievement of your goals and objectives and learn new ways of thinking and new ways of looking at things. I do this by a process called reframing. For example, if you say that you never get anything right. I would respectfully challenge you and say NEVER! I am sure there was a time when you got something right so let's see what you did then and how we can implement those strategies in this situation.

Coaching is a model of learning and potentiality which focuses on the future and its achievable goals and outcomes. It is about understanding the past as a framework for the present and creating a better future. When appropriate I as a coach will share about my experience which is vital to the learning process.

It is both empowering and thought provoking for you to explore what is possible in your life.

The changes will amaze you as they are fast and so much fun. It focuses on actions, outcomes, and process, remembering that you as a person are perfectly capable of best performance if only you get in touch with those capabilities. As a coach I align mentally with you and through questioning I identify the challenges, then I provide coaching to move you beyond them to create wins. In the process, you are responsible in achieving the outcomes.

Coaching is primarily to improve performance or skills and achieve a positive outcome, whereas counselling is primarily to help resolve emotional problems and conflicts in interpersonal relationships.

Consulting

I have worked as a consultant in both education and health. I worked nationally as a lead Inspector for Early Years for the Independent Schools Inspectorate (ISI). In this role I would go into schools and gather information on how that school met the health and welfare of children along with being able to meet the Early Years Foundation Curriculum. I would interview parents and children along with staff and then write up a report of my findings. At the end of the inspection, I would give this feedback to the Board and give them information on how to make improvements in areas that were of concern to me.

I also worked for Montessori Evaluation and Accreditation Board (MEAB) as an assessor to assess whether the schools I was visiting had the credibility and know-how to be awarded with recognition and status of holding the plaque for being an accredited Montessori school/nursery.

In health I worked as a safeguarding consultant to ensure that health care settings had policies and processes in place to protect children from harm.

Consulting is directive in its approach and usually involves going into an organisation and giving advice, guidance, and support. At the end of the process a written report will be provided. Consultants are recognised in their fields, who either sell their expert advice or preform their expert actions to complete a task on behalf of their clients. Consultants are hired to solve problems. With consulting, you have considerable control over the process and virtually no control over the results. Consultants normally seek and take credit for the work done or achievements. Consultants must maintain their superior/expert position and rarely form a close relationship with their clients. Consultants rarely affect the personal improvement of their organisations they provide their services to.

Mentoring

Mentors focus on providing mentees with advice and wisdom gathered through experience and knowledge when the mentee asks for their insight. Mentors can be a library of human knowledge in a particular area of life that they have gained expertise such as in nursing, education, health, or business. Mentors normally focus on providing knowledge, understanding and direction, but have been known to help in the improvement of the person they are mentoring thus allowing the mentee to become the expert. Mentors advise, guide and support.

Whereas in coaching we rarely offer advise as to what to do – I coach you in HOW to utilise your own capabilities by discovering and utilising your intrinsic sometimes hidden abilities. I like to release your untapped potential. I can assist you in maximising those abilities and so, to make possible for you to take the actions necessary to achieve the desired results. Coaching is a non-directive approach and is facilitative in nature as it is my belief that YOU have all the answers inside of you already. I will just help you in finding what is right for YOU.

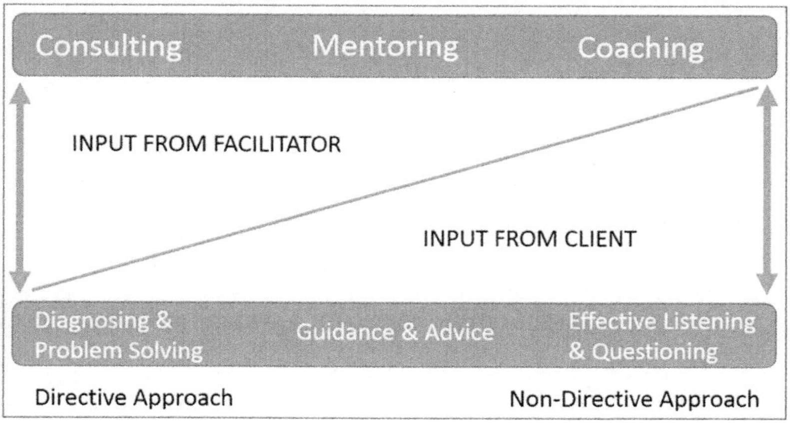

Figure 9: The Consulting/Mentoring/Coaching Spectrum

Coaching Models

There are many coaching models and approaches used in coaching. I will outline five of them.

1. The CLEAR model developed by Peter Hawkins in the 1980s. It stands for Contract, Listen, Explore, Action, and Review.
2. The STEPPA model created by Dr. Angus McLeod. This stands for Subject, Target identification, Emotion, Perception, Plan/Place and Action.
3. The OSCAR model described by Gilbert and Whittleworth in 2002 and stands for Outcome, Situation, Choices, Action and Review.
4. The ASPIRE model created by Tracy Driscoll, a 5-stage process of Explore, Inspire, Create, Act and Reflect.
5. The LEAP model created by Judith Tolhurst which stands for Looking at goals, Exploring reality, Analysing Possibilities and Panning action.

My preferred model of choice is the GROW model.

G = Goal,
R = Reality/Resources available to you,
O = Options/Obstacles,
W = Way forward/willing to do to move you one step closer to your goal.

Principles of using this technique

Coaching is about helping you to learn, rather than teaching you to do something. It focusses on future possibilities, not past failures. I come to the sessions with no preconceived ideas. When I work with you, I get you to begin with the end in mind. This principle is taken from the book written by Stephen Covey, *The 7 Habits of Highly Successful People*. If you haven't read this book yet, I would highly recommend you do. Goal setting is key to success.

Benefits of mentoring and coaching:

1. Increased self-awareness
2. Increased confidence
3. Resilience
4. Collaboration/communication
5. Learning to self-reflect/deeper level of learning
6. Learn from other's experience
7. Self-efficacy
8. Empowerment
9. Work-life balance
10. Focus and clarity
11. Improved performance
12. Goal achievement

When I start working with you, I carry out an intake session, this includes personality analysis, values elicitation, and a baseline assessment of where you are in your life and business using a coaching tool called 'The Wheel of Success'.

I have 3 packages of coaching, 3, 6 and 12 months. Helen decided to buy my top coaching package – The Ultimate Success Package a 12-month programme.

Case Study

Helen sought me out as she was having trouble in her business. She wanted more clarity and to grow her business but didn't know how to achieve this. When we did the wheel of success together, she scored 4-5 out of 10 in the 8 areas of her business that she identified and wanted to focus on. The 8 included vision, communication, clarity, sales, teamwork, delegation, trust, and leadership. These areas usually arise out of the values elicitation exercise. I coached her in the aspects of her business. Having worked with me for a year she had increased her score to 10 in all but one area of her business.

The Wheel of Success Tool

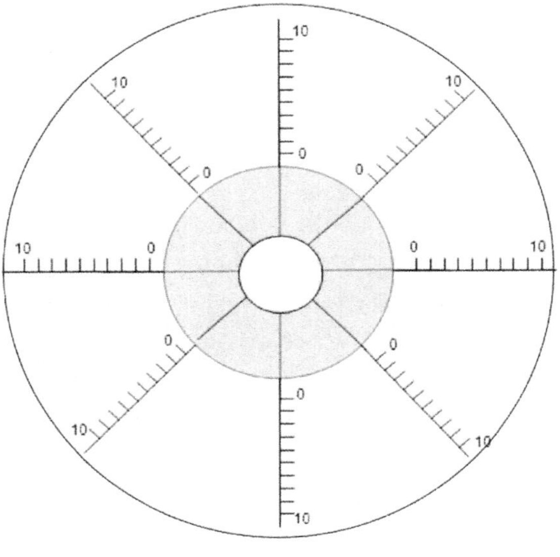

Figure 10: The Wheel of Success

I believe that every good coach should have their own coach and be registered with an accredited organisation. I have been a member of the European Mentoring Coaching Council since I qualified as a coach. It is also worth saying that you do not have to be qualified to set up as a coach in the UK and currently there are no regulations surrounding it. If you are thinking about taking on a coach, please do check with their past clients to see if they are the right fit for you and that they can get you the results that you desire. I have coached many hundreds of clients over the last decade, I am an award-winning coach from my work in the NHS. I still work as a volunteer coach for the NHS Leadership Academy as I like to give back and help my fellow nurses to succeed.

I have had my own coach since qualifying as a coach and that is what has allowed me to have the success that I have created in my life and my career. I have invested thousands of pounds in both mentoring and coaching as I feel the best investment for your business is investing in you.

Summary

In this chapter we have looked at the difference between mentoring, coaching, therapy, and consulting. I have touched on the different approaches to coaching. I shared a success story where I used one of the many tools I implement in my coaching, the 'Wheel of Success'. I finished off with the benefits it brings in helping you achieve success in life and business.

CHAPTER 9

The Power of the Mastermind

"Accountability closes the gap between intention and results."

Sandy Gallagher

Introduction

I have never been very good at asking for help from other people. I guess I just always thought that people are busy, and I didn't want to bother them. I always try and put myself in other people's shoes as I know how busy life is for everyone trying to juggle so many things in their life, with work, family, business, and hobbies. But this was a decision that held me back and caused me much distress. It's so much harder doing things on your own and trying to figure out stuff yourself it is very time consuming. I learned this the hard way. Asking for help is not a weakness, it is a strength, and this is what I have learned over the course of my life and business.

When I first went into business 13 years ago, I struggled with everything; I had to learn the hard way and made many mistakes. It's unfortunate that most people think they must learn in this way but there is an alternative and that's the power of working with other people and leveraging their knowledge, skills and experience.

There are different ways that you can achieve this type of support and help. But the two main ways are in having an accountability partner/buddy or join a mastermind group.

Accountability

Accountability is an important priority in the life of truly successful individuals. This is a statement made by the Proctor Gallagher Institute in their programme 'Thinking into Results' (TIR). Accountability is the glue that cements the commitment to your result.

I know from my own experience that accountability is crucial to success in life and in your business. As mentioned previously, I have always had mentors and coaches in my life, as I believe this is what keeps me moving forward by holding me accountable. When we set our intention in a group situation, we are far more likely to follow through on that intention if we have to report back to someone. That is human nature; we don't like to let people down.

What I have learned from the various membership and courses that I have taken is that the ones that produce the best results have an accountability buddy system in place. This can be on a one-to-one basis or in a group. Both bring many benefits, the main being:

1. It helps build valuable relationships
2. It helps in productivity
3. It provides useful insights
4. It helps increase learning
5. You get the expertise and experience of all the group's members (group)

My own experience is proof that a buddy system works and gets you results. I had been working with the same buddy one-on-one for over a year as part of a business mentorship training programme. Working with him, I was able to achieve 3.5K in a single month from 4 sales. Out of all the members within that membership -- which exceeded a hundred members -- I hit number one in that month for my drive and commitment to my business. I don't think I would have achieved that without having an accountability buddy. I also committed to a group accountability session every month within the same membership. If you want results this is the way to achieve it.

How does an accountability buddy system work?

If you belong to an accountability group, there will be a leader of that group. They will be responsible for the time keeping and asking the questions. It is important that all members of the group get equal time allotted to them to make it equitable. You always want to aim for a win: win; if people don't get an opportunity to have their time, this will result in a win: lose for those members who may not want to continue with the group. The role of the leader is crucial in ensuring that this does not happen.

In many situations there will be an agreement that is put in place by the group members, and all will sign it so there is an understanding of the expectation of the group.

The time allotted will depend on the size of the group, as a group leader I will make sure that all participants have equal time to share. I do not advise on any more than 6 in a group and no longer than 2 hours. I currently belong to a group where there are 3 of us and we meet monthly for an hour. We have 20 mins each to share.

Procedure

The leader will be the one who asks the questions. They will delegate the time -keeping to a second member of the group. The third person will be the note taker and then we rotate the roles. In this way we are all equal in the process.

Step 1

I start with the wins since we last met. This allows the energy to be positive at the start of the session.

Step 2

Look at the goals set from the previous session and check in to see if they have been achieved. The point of the group is to hold people accountable so there is a fine balance between guilt tripping them if they have not achieved the goal and offering supportive challenge as to what got in the way.

Step 3

We look at the challenges that may be getting in the way of progress and what the group can do to help or find the solution to the challenge.

Step 4

We then set our goals for the next session.

What is a mastermind group?

In essence, a mastermind group is a group of peers who meet to give each other advice and support. It is like an accountability group but a bit more fluid in my experience with a less structured approach.

Mastermind groups can also involve brainstorming, educational presentations an even discussing personal issues. Many people think of these groups as mastermind classes, but they are not a class. There is no single teacher or leader, it's co-owned and co-created by the group. In other words, a mastermind is a meeting of minds. It is a place where you can speak the truth and expect the same in return.

I have just completed a year-long mentorship training programme with Joel Bauer. Joel is known as the 'mentors' mentor', and he is an expert in helping business owners present and close. I am still part of the mastermind group, and we meet monthly.

I am now in another mentorship programme with my current mentor Kim Calvert. This mentorship programme has helped me grow in faith and awareness to a whole new level. It started with a 6-month programme Called Thinking into Results (TIR) this included 12 lessons.

1. A Worthy Ideal – Setting and Achieving Worthy Goals.
2. The Knowing/Doing Gap – Understanding the Knowing/Doing Gap.
3. Your Infinite Mind – Using Your Mind to Get the Results You Want.
4. The Secret Genie – Unlocking the Secret.
5. Thinking Into Results – The Trick to Staying in Charge No matter the Circumstances.
6. Environment Is but Our Looking Glass – Creating the Environment and Team That You Want.
7. Trample the Terror Barrier – Identifying and Avoiding the Land Mine That Will Sabotage Your Success.
8. The Power of Praxis – Aligning You with You So We All Win.

9. The Magic Word – The Magic of Attitude.
10. The Most Valuable Person – The Leader is the Most Valuable Person.
11. Leaving Everyone with The Impression of Increase.
12. The Secret of the Mind - The Secret to Increasing the Power of Your Mind.

The twelve lessons have made a huge impact on my life and the decisions that I am making in my life and business. This program focusses on changing your mindset and moving you towards your 'C' type goals. Success is about 95% mindset and 5% strategy. Many business owners get this the wrong way around.

The concept of the mastermind itself can be traced back to Napoleon Hill, the author of *Think and Grow Rich*. In this classic book, Hill discusses the use of mastermind groups among successful American companies during that time in the 1930s. He described mastermind groups as two or more people coming together with the sole purpose of solving a specific problem.

> *"No two minds ever come together without thereby creating a third, invisible intangible force, which may be likened to a third mind [the master mind]."*
>
> —*Napoleon Hill*

There are seven 'Mastermind Principles' that TIR have produced that I would like to share with you.

- **I release** - I released myself to the mastermind because I am strong, and I have others to help me.
- **I believe** - I believe the combined intelligence of the mastermind creates a wisdom far beyond my own.

- **I understand** - I understand that I will more easily create positive results in my life, and I am open to looking at myself, my problems and opportunities from another point of view.
- **I decide** - I decide to release my desire and total interest to the mastermind and I am open to accepting new possibilities.
- **I forgive** - I forgive myself for mistakes I have made. I also forgive others who have hurt me in the past so I can move into the future with a clean slate.
- **I ask** - I ask the mastermind to hear what I really want; my goals, my dreams and my desires and I hear my mastermind partners supporting me in my fulfilment.
- **I accept** - I know, I relax, I accept, believing that the working power of the mastermind will respond to my every need. I'm grateful knowing that it is so.

The benefits of the mastermind group are having a level of accountability which will make all the difference in your life and business to move you forward. To succeed you need to have the right mindset, a mission, and then make the moves.

Summary

This chapter focused on the power, benefits and dynamics of an accountability buddy or group to support you in your journey. It also reviewed how a mastermind group works in moving you forward to success.

Conclusion

Life and business are a roller coaster. This book has taken you through some of mine, and the decisions that I have taken to move me forward in life. I was told that I wasn't clever enough to go to university or get a degree. I believed that and allowed that limiting decision to hold me back from what I wanted to be. I lived in the shadows for 25 years afraid of everything, not wanting my voice to be heard as I thought I wasn't worthy of being listened to. I had a fixed mindset and didn't think I could change.

I had a small glimmer of faith to enable me to start my first business in 2004 because the desire to be with my children was my mission. I didn't know the HOW I just had blind faith that I would succeed. Yes, it was hard, and I made many mistakes, but I learned, and I course-corrected along the way. I made the moves, and I kept on moving forward. I have never looked back.

Life and business can knock you but with the right mindset you get up again and keep going. Many people give up as they don't have the right mindset. I must admit that my first two businesses nearly broke me physically and emotionally. But now I have the resources to deal with setbacks. I just take the learning and forget the rest.

But the turning point for me was finding myself and moving into my personal development journey. Every success confirmed to me that I had huge potential that was untapped, just like you have. I have grown so much as a person. I have more confidence and belief in myself. With every success came more belief and conviction that I AM ENOUGH. I made the decision after studying for my PhD for 3 years that I did not need another degree or the title of having a doctorate. I have all the knowledge, skills and experience I need right now for what I do, and I love to serve other people to help them realise and know this: YOU are good enough, too.

I hope that my story has empowered you to believe in yourself and your ability to succeed. You only fail if you give up. If you implement the tools and exercises in this book, it will help you to shift some of your blocks and barriers that may be holding you back from being the best version of yourself.

Make the decision today to keep moving forward. Don't let the past define you, take the learning and forget the rest. Continue to learn and grow and strive to be a better version of yourself every day. Make your dreams a reality. Don't let anything or anyone hold you back and believe in yourself and your ability to succeed.

It all starts with a DECISION.

BONUS:

Chapter One

CHAPTER 10

Who Do You Think You Are?

Personality Tool - Myers Briggs Type Indicator (MBTI)

We need to understand ourselves before we can understand others. It is important that we understand our personality and what makes us who we are, we are all unique and have gifts to share with the world. When I work with you as part of my intake session, I will always ask for permission carry out a personality analysis using either DISC Assessment (Dominance, Influence, Steadiness Conscientiousness) or Myers Briggs Type Indicator (MBTI) which most people are familiar with.

The MBTI questionnaire assesses preferences. There are eight in total that lie within four dimensions. These being:

1. *Extraversion or Introversion* – Where do you prefer to get information and focus your 'energy' or attention. Extroverts get their energy from being around people. Introverts get energised or recharged from being on their own and enjoying quite time.

2. *Sensing or Intuition* – What kind of information you prefer to gather and trust.
   Sensing people prefer information coming from the five senses, focus on what is real, they like facts, specifics, and value practical applications. Whereas intuitive people prefer information coming in from association; they like the big picture and ideas, focusing more on what might be. They value imagination and insight.
3. *Thinking or Feeling* – What processes do you prefer to use in making decisions?
   Thinking people prefer to make decisions based on logic and objectivity, they seek objective truth and focus on the task. Whereas feeling people prefer to make decisions based on values and personal convictions. They understand other people's points of view and seek harmony. Their focus is on relationship.
4. *Judging or Perceiving* – How you prefer to deal with the world around you, 'your lifestyle'.
   Judges prefer to live in a planned organised manner; they enjoy bringing things to a closure and being decisive. They tend to avoid stressful last-minute rushes. Perceivers, on the other hand prefer life in a spontaneous and adaptable manner, like keeping options open and being curious. They feel energised by last-minute pressures.

When I coach you, this information is crucial in being able to adapt to your preferences. If there is a mismatch this will cause some friction in the coaching relationship or any relationship whether it be a partner, friend, work colleague or boss. We need to put ourselves in the other person's shoes and see it from their point of view. I do this through my training as an NLP practitioner using a technique called perceptual positions.

NLP Tool # 6 – Perceptual Positions

This is the ability to see things from another's perspective. There are three positions.

First position–This is looking at the world from your own point of view. You are totally associated in your own body and not thinking of anyone else's point of view. It's your own reality with all your own values, beliefs, and opinions.

Second position – from this position you are considering how it would look, feel, and sound for another person. You are looking through the other person's eyes, appreciating the other person's point of view (empathy). It is stepping into someone else's shoes. How does it feel for them? This position is about appreciating and understanding their world; you don't have to agree with it.

Third position – from here you are seeing the world from an outsider point of view, from a dissociated position as an independent observer, someone with no personal involvement in the situation. You can observe the 'system' or the connections and the relationship between the first and the second position (this is often this is my position as the coach). How would this look to someone who is not involved? This creates an objective and an opportunity to evaluate some useful choices in a difficult situation.

Application

Often when we lack confidence, we are so wrapped up in how others perceive us that we lose sight of what's going on for other people. We are operating from the first position, it's all about me.

This is because we are almost always in a flight, fight or freeze response in social situations. It's not that we are a selfish person, not at all, we are just so focused on trying to quiet that inner voice that is telling us that we are not good enough, clever enough, funny enough, whatever it is that our negative beliefs and limiting decisions have been running in our mind. We have told ourselves this repeatedly over the years. We just go into automatic pilot as it is deeply rooted in our subconscious mind. We are not listening to what the other person is saying because we are trying to think of an answer to say that will be intelligent and appeal to the other person that we are talking to.

If we stop and take the focus off ourselves and move into the second position, then we can start focusing on the other person. They might be feeling the same as you. Just be yourself, relax; you can't think clearly if you are in a heightened state of fear. All logic goes out the window. Remember, they are just like you – a mother, daughter, brother, son.

TOP TIP: Find common ground and talk about, such as family that will relax both of you. Family is a great place to start as everyone knows their family well and you can connect on a human level.

BONUS:
Chapter Two

CHAPTER 11

Recognise Your Saboteurs

What are saboteurs?

Saboteurs are the voices in our head that generate negative feelings in the way we respond to the challenges of life. They are automatic patterns or strategies in our mind that are our natural responses that we revert to how we think, feel, and respond. They are the contribute to your stress, anxiety, self-doubt, frustration, restlessness, and unhappiness in life. They sabotage your performance, wellbeing, and relationships.

Let me introduce you to the saboteurs. There are ten in total:

1. The Judge – known as the master saboteur, and we all have this one even, if we don't recognise or admit to it.

The remaining nine are known as the accomplice saboteurs.

2. Avoider
3. Controller
4. Hyper-Achiever
5. Hyper-Rational
6. Hyper-Vigilant
7. Pleaser

8. Restless
9. Stickler
10. Victim

Avoider – this saboteur will focus on the positive and be pleasant in an extreme way. They avoid difficult and unpleasant tasks and conflicts. This is the type of person who procrastinates and as a result is never able to accomplish anything.

Controller – this saboteur is anxiety-based; this type of person will need to take charge and control situations and people in order to satisfy their own needs. It is characterised by high anxiety and impatience if they are not able to remain in control.

Hyper-Achiever – this saboteur is dependent on constant performance and achievement for self-respect and self-validation. They are continuously striving for perfection; every time they achieve a qualification or title, they are quickly discount it and in need of more.

Hyper-Rational – this saboteur is intense an exclusively focused on rationally processing everything around them including relationships. This type of person can be perceived as uncaring, unfeeling, or intellectually arrogant.

Hyper-Vigilant – this saboteur has a continuous, intense anxiety about all the dangers and what could go wrong in their life or in any given situation. Their vigilance can never rest, and they may present in a persistent state of worry and doubt.

Pleaser – this saboteur indirectly tries to gain acceptance and affection by helping, pleasing, rescuing, or flattering others. They lose sight of their own needs and become resentful as a result.

Restless – this saboteur is constantly restless and in search of greater excitement and the next activity that is going to give them a buzz. They are constantly busy, and they often go from one thing to another never completing anything. They are the course junkie; they are rarely at peace or content with their current activity.

Stickler – this saboteur is always aiming for perfection. They need to have law and order in everything they do but they take it too far. They are anxious trying to make too many things perfect and this stops them from moving forward.

Victim – this saboteur is emotional and temperamental, and they are wanting constant attention and affection from others. They have an extreme focus on internal feelings, particularly the painful ones. They are pessimistic in their outlook on life, and they have a martyr streak in them.

It is worth recognising what your saboteurs are and if you are interested to discover your own, please go to www.positiveintelligence.com for a FREE assessment. This work has been developed by Shirzad Chamine. I would thoroughly recommend this course if you feel that your saboteurs are controlling your life.

My Saboteurs

I learned that my top three saboteurs are pleaser, hyper-achiever, and restless.

I recognise all of these in myself, and I see how they have controlled me throughout my life. I have always wanted to please others since I was a child. I think this is due to my personality.

I am a very caring and empathic person that's why I went into nursing, and I tend to put other people before myself. I have always had difficulty in saying no to people, which means that I often had very little time left for me as I came last on the list. But this led me to feeling resentful; now I have learned to put myself first and take time out and recharge.

Since my experience at school and being told that I was stupid, I have always tried to prove to myself that this was not the case. Therefore, I have attended multiple courses and studied throughout my life, in order to gain another qualification or certificate to make me feel better, but they never did. I always needed to go on and get another piece of paper. Thankfully this is no longer the case.

My final saboteur is restless. I feel that this is associated with being a hyper-achiever. I get bored very easily and I've never stayed in a job for longer than two years. I am continuously wanting to do something else and move on to the next challenge. This, of course, can be exhausting as you are always starting over.

How to manage the saboteurs

There is a solution to dealing with your saboteurs and that's by increasing your sage characteristics (positive self). You address the saboteurs by building up new neural pathways in the brain by doing daily training to develop the sage characteristics that are found in the six-week foundation course, which works on mental fitness. If you decide to investigate this further the course looks at three things to develop your Positive Intelligence (PQ) through the App that you download once, you sign up for the program. The App tracks your progress when you carry out the daily exercises throughout the day. It helps build up your positive self.

1. Self-command muscle
2. Saboteur interceptor muscle
3. Sage muscle - there are 5 sage powers: empathise, explore, innovate, navigate, and activate.

The process weakens your saboteurs and strengthens your self-command and 5 sage powers.

Acknowledgements

This book would not have been possible to write without the knowledge, skills and experience of my amazing book coach, Mirav Tarkka, who encouraged me and kept moving me forward towards my end goal of becoming a #1 best-selling author.

To all the other authors in my group who, on a weekly basis, I shared this journey during fun sessions together.

To all those who read my taster chapters and gave me reviews.

To the editor who corrected all my grammar and spelling mistakes.

To the graphic designer who did my amazing cover.

To my launching team.

And lastly to my Irish teacher who I have learned to forgive as she has motivated me to be the person that I am today.

LEGAL DISCLAIMER - A New Dawning

The entire content of *A New Dawning*, must be considered as exclusively informative and cannot in any way be understood as a substitute, alternative or supplementary of professional opinions or medical consultations, nor refer to specific individual cases, for which we invite you to consult your own attending physician and / or recognized specialists. The contents of *A New Dawning* are for informational purposes only and should not be intended to treat, diagnose, prevent, or treat any ailment or disease. The author of this work declines any responsibility for any consequences deriving from a use of its contents other than merely informative.

Nothing contained in this work constitutes or intends to constitute a suggestion of any nature. If the reader of *A New Dawning* feels the need for advice in relation to any topic, you are invited to contact a qualified professional in the specific field.

If the reader of *A New Dawning* suspects or is aware of having or having had or is being exposed to problems, disturbances and / or physical or psychological illnesses they must seek on appropriate medical treatment recommended by a professional of their own trust.

Despite the scrupulous care used in the preparation of *A New Dawning,* drawn up with the utmost accuracy and diligence, it is not possible to ensure that the information contained within it is free from errors, omissions or inaccuracies.

Ann Guindi disclaims any liability, direct and indirect, towards readers, regarding inaccuracies, errors, omissions, or damages deriving from the contents.

The author of *A New Dawning* cannot guarantee the users of the book to obtain the same results of personal, character growth, psychological, motivational, physical or any other nature or denomination on a par with as set out in this work.

Within *A New Dawning* the ideas of consultants and experts are cited and hosted which in a free form, not constituting what they affirmed an opinion of a professional or similar nature, offered their contribution for information purposes only, without any presumption or willingness to place oneself above the recognized traditional medical system. It is at the free discretion of the user of *A New Dawning* and its absolute responsibility for any willingness to follow or replicate some of the advice proposed therein or to contact other competent personnel, according to your own beliefs, knowledge, habits and wills.

Everything included within *A New Dawning* must always be understood as the subjective opinion of the author, given that these considerations can also run counter to the precepts of knowledge taught in universities and / or in the scientific world and therefore go there considered as simple expressions or controversies of a personal and in any case non-professional nature, having to make exclusive reference to / and reliance solely on traditional and recognized fields of knowledge.

Printed in Great Britain
by Amazon

15684362R00092